The Complete Ninja Speedi Cookbook for Beginners

Simple Air Fry, Bake, Roast, Sear, and More Recipes for Anyone to Cook with Ninja Speedi Rapid Cooker & Air Fryer

Kerry Wilburn

© Copyright 2023 – All Rights Reserved

This document is geared towards providing exact and reliable information with regards to the topic and issue covered. The publication is sold with the idea that the publisher is not required to render accounting, officially permitted, or otherwise, qualified services. If advice is necessary, legal, or professional, a practiced individual in the profession should be ordered. -From a Declaration of Principles which was accepted and approved equally by a Committee of the American Bar Association and a Committee of Publishers and Associations. In no way is it legal to reproduce, duplicate, or transmit any part of this document in either electronic means or in printed format. Recording of this publication is strictly prohibited and any storage of this document is not allowed unless with written permission from the publisher.

All rights reserved. The information provided herein is stated to be truthful and consistent, in that any liability, in terms of inattention or otherwise, by any usage or abuse of any policies, processes, or directions contained within is the solitary and utter responsibility of the recipient reader.

Under no circumstances will any legal responsibility or blame be held against the publisher for any reparation, damages, or monetary loss due to the information herein, either directly or indirectly. Respective authors own all copyrights not held by the publisher.

The information herein is offered for informational purposes solely, and is universal as so. The presentation of the information is without contract or any type of guarantee assurance. The trademarks that are used are without any consent, and the publication of the trademark is without permission or backing by the trademark owner.

All trademarks and brands within this book are for clarifying purposes only and are the owned by the owners themselves, not affiliated with this document.

CONTENTS

1   Introduction

12   4-Week Meal Plan

14   Chapter 1 Breakfast Recipes

27   Chapter 2 Vegetable and Sides Recipes

39   Chapter 3 Snacks and Appetizers Recipes

51   Chapter 4 Poultry Recipes

61   Chapter 5 Pork, Beef and Lamb Recipes

75   Chapter 6 Seafood Recipes

85   Chapter 7 Dessert Recipes

98   Conclusion

99   Appendix 1 Air Fryer Cooking Chart

100   Appendix 2 Measurement Conversion Chart

101   Appendix 3 Recipes Index

Introduction

The Ninja Speedi is an advanced kitchen appliance that provides maximum cooking flexibility. With its combination of air frying, steaming, and both functions, you can create Speedi Meals featuring a grain, vegetable, and protein that cook simultaneously on two levels. Plus, it has an array of settings for everything from Steam & Crisp to Slow Cook and Sous Vide. The Speedi is designed for ultimate convenience, with a lever on the lid to switch between Air Fry and Rapid Cooker modes and a touchscreen to control all 12 functions. With the Ninja Speedi, you can cook confidently like a professional chef.

The Speedi air fryer and multicooker are a great addition to any kitchen. It easily fits under a cabinet with the lid down, but when used, it should be pulled out onto the countertop to provide enough space to raise the lid. This intuitive appliance comes with a large removable cooking pot and a flat crisper tray and is backed by a comprehensive manual and additional resources. For a hassle-free cooking experience, the Speedi Meal Builder provides a range of suggested combinations of food and cooking times. Plus, the accompanying pamphlet and booklet provide instructions on how to make Speedi Meals, along with recipes, color photos, and cooking charts. Professional cooks and home chefs can benefit from the convenience and versatility of the Speedi, making it a great choice for adults looking for an efficient and stress-free cooking experience.

What Is Ninja Speedi?

The Speedi is the perfect air fryer and multicooker for any kitchen. With the lid down, the Speedi fits easily under a cabinet. When in use, however, it needs to be pulled forward on the countertop to provide ample space for raising the lid. This Ninja appliance has a large removable cooking pot and a flat crisper tray. Plus, the Speedi manual and pamphlet provide instructions on how to cook Speedi Meals, along with a booklet of recipes, color photos, and cooking charts. What's more, you can access the Speedi Meal Builder online, which suggests various combinations of foods and cooking times. With the Speedi, professional-level cooking results are within your reach.

Feature of Ninja Speedi

1. Speedi Meals function provides a quick and easy way to prepare a delicious meal for up to four in as little as 15 minutes.
2. With the 6-qt. Capacity, you can combine base, vegetables, and protein to create a wholesome one-pot meal that will satisfy the entire family. Let the Speedi Meals function take the guesswork out of meal planning, and enjoy a meal in no time.
3. 12-in-1 Functionality: Get maximum cooking flexibility with Rapid Cooker mode - unlocking Speedi Meals, Steam & Crisp, Steam & Bake, Steam, and Proof options. Then, switch to Air Fry mode and unlock a new world of culinary possibilities - including

Air Fry, Bake/Roast, Air Broil, Dehydrate, Sear & Sauté, Slow Cook, and Sous Vide functions. With our professional-grade 12-in-1 appliance, you'll have the power to easily make all of your favorite dishes.

4. The Rapid Cooking System allows you to quickly create moisture with steam, caramelize, and crisp with air fry technology simultaneously in one pot – for restaurant-worthy results. Take advantage of the Rapid Cooker mode and enjoy professional-level meals at home.

5. Discover the ultimate cooking convenience with SmartSwitch functionality. Easily switch between Air Fry mode and Rapid Cooker mode to unlock a world of delicious possibilities. With this professional-grade feature, you'll be able to master any dish easily and give your meals an extra kick of flavor. Enjoy the convenience of SmartSwitch today and unlock the power of your kitchen!

6. With the Ninja Speedi Meal Builder, you can unlock thousands of delicious and customizable recipes tailored to the ingredients already in your fridge or

pantry. No matter what type of meal you're craving, our easy-to-use tool will help you create the perfect dish quickly and professionally. So what are you waiting for? Start building your speedi meal today!

7. Air frying is a healthier way to prepare meals - up to 75% less fat when using the air fry function compared to traditional deep frying. We've tested it against hand-cut, deep-fried French fries, and the results speak for themselves. Enjoy the same delicious taste without the guilt - air fry your meals today and start eating healthier!

8. Speedi Cleanup offers a fast and easy solution to your cleanup needs. Our nonstick pot and crisper tray are dishwasher-safe, making the cleanup process a breeze. With this professional-grade kitchenware, you can enjoy quick and efficient cleaning in no time.

Main Functions of Ninja Speedi

The Ninja Speedi is a revolutionary appliance that comes with 12 amazing cooking functions. All functionality is best for delicious food making with perfection.

Rapid Cooker

Speedi Meals:

Speedi Meals provide an easy and efficient way to make two-part meals with just one touch. With the Ninja Speedi, you can make a delicious meal in no time, every time. Professional chefs and home cooks alike can now enjoy the convenience of a fast and tasty meal with the simple press of a button. Make meals easy with the Ninja Speedi, and give yourself the time to savor each delicious bite.

Steam & Crisp:

Create a combination of juicy and crisp results with the perfect balance of moisture and crunch. Professional chefs and home cooks alike will appreciate the convenience and ease of use that Steam & Crisp provides. Enjoy the confidence of having perfectly cooked food every time - juicy on the inside, crisp on the outside. Enjoy eating healthier with less fat and fewer calories.

Introduction | 3

Steam & Crisp Bake:

Create fluffier cakes and quick bread faster and with less fat using the STEAM & CRISP BAKE Function. This professional-grade baking solution allows you to bake your creations with greater precision and control while saving time and energy. Enjoy delicious, light, fluffy cakes and bread cooked to perfection with less fat. Experience the perfect baking results every time with Ninja speedi.

Steam:

The ninja Speedi Steam mode helps you gently cook delicate foods at a high temperature. This professional-grade cooking method ensures that your dishes are perfectly cooked with minimal effort. With this advanced technology, you can trust that your meals will be cooked precisely as you intended.

Proof:

Ninja Speedi creates the perfect environment for the dough to rest and rise, providing professional bakers with the ideal conditions to craft their delicious creations. With its advanced temperature and humidity controls, Ninja Speedi ensures that dough can rest and rise efficiently and consistently, giving bakers the confidence to produce incredible results time and time again.

Air Fry/Stovetop

Sear/Sauté:

Transform your Ninja Speedi into a professional stovetop with the perfect tools for browning meats, sautéing veggies, simmering sauces, and more. With the Ninja Speedi, you can now enjoy restaurant-quality cooking right in the comfort of your own home. Bring gourmet-level results to your kitchen with ease, speed, and precision.

Slow Cook:

Cook your food to perfection with the Ninja speedi Slow Cooker Mode. This innovative mode allows you to cook your meals at a lower temperature for longer, meaning you don't have to worry about being in the kitchen all day. With the Ninja speedi Slow Cooker Mode, you can do whatever you need to while your food cooks perfectly. Enjoy high-quality meals without having to sacrifice your time!

Sous Vide:

Sous vide, a French term meaning "under vacuum," is a precise cooking technique that involves vacuum-sealing food in a bag, then cooking it to a very exact temperature in a water bath. This cooking method ensures that you get consistently restaurant-quality meals every time. With sous vide, you can control the temperature to get perfect results every time. High-end restaurants have been using sous vide cooking for years to guarantee that each dish is cooked to the ideal level of doneness. With Speedi, you can enjoy restaurant-quality meals at home with perfect results each time.

Air Fry:

The AIR FRY Function is perfect for those who want to stay healthy and fit but still enjoy delicious fried foods. With minimal to no oil, you can enjoy your favorite fried foods without worrying about the extra calories. The AIR FRY Function lets you enjoy your favorite fried foods without feeling guilty. With the AIR FRY Function, you can indulge in fried foods while maintaining a healthy, fit lifestyle.

Bake/Roast

Bake/Roast is the perfect solution for quickly and easily roasting meats, vegetables, and more. This Function turns your unit into an efficient roaster oven that preserves the flavor and texture of your food. Whether you're looking to cook for a large group or want to meal prep for the week ahead, this is the perfect solution. With bake/roast, you can easily enjoy delicious, perfectly cooked baked treats and tender roasted meats.

Broil:

This Function offers a unique way to add texture, colour, and crispness to your food. From melting cheese on burgers and pasta to caramelizing sugar on top of the pudding and Brulee, you can now create healthy and delicious meals that are also crispy and caramelized. With this advanced technique, the possibilities are almost endless – allowing you to experiment with various recipes and make the most out of your ingredients. Make your meals healthier and tastier with this professional cooking innovation!

Dehydrate:

The Ninja Speedi is the perfect appliance for healthy and delicious dehydrated snacks. With its advanced dehydrating Function, you can enjoy the best dry food without needing expensive dehydrators. This Function also eliminates the need for overpriced or complicated dehydrators in your kitchen, making it the ideal choice for professionals and health-conscious individuals.

Experience the convenience and quality of Ninja Speedi for your dehydrated food needs.

Buttons and User Guide of Ninja Speedi

Operating Buttons Smartswitch: Operate your SmartSwitch with ease! Move up and down to switch between Rapid Cooker and Air Fry/Stovetop mode. All available functions for each mode will light up for easy identification. With this intuitive system, you can cook easily and precisely - making meals for you and your family faster and easier than ever. Unlock the potential of your kitchen today with the SmartSwitch!

Center Arrows: Using the SmartSwitch, the center arrows provide an easy way to scroll through the available options and select your desired Function. You can quickly and conveniently access your needed features with a few clicks, making your experience more efficient and professional.

Left Arrows: Use the up and down arrows to the left of the display to adjust the cooking temperature for optimal results. Professional and home cooks will

benefit from this intuitive and easy-to-use feature.

Right Arrows: Use the up/down arrows to the right of the display to adjust the cooking time for optimal results easily. Professional chefs and home cooks can benefit from this convenient feature to create delicious meals.

Start/Stop Button: Press the button to start cooking. To stop the current cooking function, press the button again while the unit is cooking. This is a professional and reliable way to control your cooking.

Power: With the press of the POWER button, you can quickly and easily shut off your unit and stop all cooking functions. This efficient solution allows adults to easily and professionally control their cooking environment.

Before First Use

1. Before using your unit, remove and discard all packaging materials, stickers, and tape.
2. Pay close attention to the operational instructions, warnings, and important safeguards to ensure the safety of yourself and your property.
3. Wash the removable pot, crisper tray, and condensation collector in warm, soapy water, then rinse and dry them thoroughly for optimal operation.

How to Clean & Maintain

For optimal performance, cleaning the Ninja Speedi thoroughly before and after every use is important. To ensure thorough cleaning, follow these steps:
1. Disconnect the main unit from power before beginning the cleaning process.
2. Wipe down the main unit and control panel with a damp cloth.
3. Place the dishwasher-safe accessories like the basket and crisper plate in the dishwasher.
4. Soak the plates in warm soapy water to remove tough food residues.
5. Dry all parts with a towel or air dry.
Following these steps, you can ensure that your Ninja

Speedi is properly cleaned and ready to deliver optimal performance.

Ninja Speedi Making Skills

Using Rapid Cooker Functions

Speedi Meals:

1. Before you begin, be sure to remove the Crisper Tray from the bottom of the pot.
2. Place the liquid and ingredients according to the recipe instructions in the bottom of the pot.
3. Pull out the legs on the Crisper Tray, then place the tray in the elevated position in the pot. Next, add the ingredients to the tray as per the recipe instructions.
4. Move the SmartSwitch to the RAPID COOKER setting, then use the center arrows to select Speedi Meals. The default setting will appear on display. With the up and down arrows to the left of the display, choose a temperature from 250°F to 450°F in increments of 10 or 15 degrees.
5. Use the arrows to the right of the display to adjust the cooking time in 1-minute increments, up to a maximum of 30 minutes.

6. Press START/STOP to begin cooking.
7. The display will show progress bars, indicating that the unit is building steam. Once the appropriate steam level is reached, the timer will begin counting down.
8. When the cooking time reaches zero, the unit will beep and display "End." If your food requires more cooking time, use the up arrows to the right of the display to increase the cooking time.

Steam & Crisp:

Follow these steps to use your SmartSwitch RAPID COOKER for cooking with steam and crispiness:

1. Gather all the ingredients according to your recipe.
2. Move the SmartSwitch to the RAPID COOKER. Use the center front arrows to select Steam & Crisp. The default setting will display.
3. Use the up and down arrows to the left of the display

to choose a temperature from 250°F to 450°F, either in 10 or 15-degree increments.
4. Use the arrows to the right of the display to adjust the cooking time from 1 to 30 minutes in 1-minute increments.
5. Press START/STOP to begin cooking. The display will show progress bars, indicating the unit is building steam.
6. The timer will begin counting down when the unit reaches the appropriate steam level.
7. When your cook time reaches zero, the unit will beep and display "End." If your food requires more time, use the up arrow to the right of the display to add additional time. The unit will skip preheating.

Steam & Bake:

1. Use your RAPID COOKER to place the Crisper Tray in the bottom position and the baking accessories on top.
2. Move the SmartSwitch to the RAPID COOKER setting, then use the center arrows to select STEAM & BAKE. The default temperature setting will display, and you can use the up and down arrows to the left to adjust the temperature from 250°F to 400°F in either 10 or 15-degree increments.
3. To adjust the cooking time, use the up and down arrows to the right of the display to set a time from 1 minute to 1 hour and 15 minutes in 1-minute

increments.

4. When you're ready to begin cooking, press START/STOP, and the display will show progress bars while the unit builds steam. When preheating is complete, the timer will start counting down.

5. When the cooking time reaches zero, the unit will beep and display "End." If additional time is needed, press the up arrow to the right of the display to add more time.

6. The unit will skip preheating for further cooking.

Steam:

1. Add the water to the bottom of the pot and place the Crisper Tray in the bottom position. Then add the ingredients of choice.

2. Set the SmartSwitch to RAPID COOKER, and use the center front arrows to select STEAM.

3. Use the up and down arrows to the right of the display to adjust the cooking time.

4. Once the cooking time is set, press START/STOP to begin cooking.

5. The unit will preheat to bring the liquid to a boil. The display will show progress bars indicating that the unit is building steam. When preheating is complete, the timer will begin counting down. The preheating animation will show until the unit reaches temperature, and then the display will switch to the timer counting down.

6. When the cooking time reaches zero, the unit will beep and display "End." Following the above steps will ensure a successful cooking experience.

Proof:

1. Place the Crisper Tray in the bottom and add dough to the baking accessory. Place the accessory on top of the tray.

2. Move the SmartSwitch to the RAPID COOKER setting, then use the center front arrows to select PROOF. The display will show the default temperature setting. Use the up and down arrows to the left of the display to choose a temperature from 90°F to 105°F in 5-degree increments.

3. Use the up and down arrows to the right of the display to adjust the proof time from 15 minutes to 4 hours in 5-minute increments.

4. Press START/STOP to begin cooking.

5. When the cooking time reaches zero, the unit will beep and display "End." Professional and knowledgeable adults should follow these steps for successful proofing.

Using Air Fryer Functions

Air Fry:

1. Start your cooking journey the right way with your Crisper Tray in the bottom position.
2. Then, add your ingredients to the pot and close the lid. Move the SmartSwitch to AIR FRY/STOVETOP, and the unit will default to AIR FRY.
3. The default temperature setting will be displayed. For precise cooking, use the up and down arrows to the left of the display to choose a temperature between 250°F and 400°F in either 10 or 15-degree increments.
4. You can also adjust the cooking time to 1 hour in minute increments using the up and down arrows to the right of the display.
5. Finally, press START/STOP to begin the cooking process.
6. When the time reaches zero, the unit will beep and display "End" to let you know it's done. With this professional and easy-to-follow guide, you can make delicious meals like a pro!

Bake/Roast:

1. It's important to place the Crisper Tray at the pot's bottom before beginning the cooking process.
2. Move the SmartSwitch to AIR FRY/STOVETOP, then use the center front arrows to select BAKE/ROAST.
3. The default temperature setting will appear, and you can use the up and down arrows to the left of the display to choose a temperature from 300°F to 400°F, with increments of either 10 or 15 degrees.
4. The up and down arrows to the right of the display can be used to adjust the cooking time up to 1 hour in 1-minute increments and from 1 hour to 4 hours in 5-minute increments.
5. Finally, press START/STOP to begin cooking. When the cooking time reaches zero, the unit will beep, and the display will read "End."
6. Follow these simple steps for the perfect bake or roast every time.

Broil:

1. To ensure optimal results, place the Crisper Tray in

Introduction | 9

an elevated position and place ingredients on the tray before closing the lid.

2. Next, move the SmartSwitch to AIR FRY/STOVETOP and use the center front arrows to select BROIL. The default temperature setting will be displayed. You can use the up and down arrows to the left of the display to set the temperature between 400°F and 450°F in 25-degree increments.

3. Using the up and down arrows to the right of the display, adjust the cooking time up to 30 minutes in 1-minute increments. Finally, press START/STOP to begin cooking.

The unit will beep and display "End" when the cooking time reaches zero.

Dehydrate:

1. Ensure the Crisper Tray is always in the bottom before beginning your dehydrating session.

2. Make sure to move the SmartSwitch to the AIR FRY/STOVETOP setting, then use the center front arrows to select DEHYDRATE. The default temperature setting will be displayed. Use the up and down arrows to the left of the display to adjust the temperature between 105°F and 195°F.

3. Utilize the up and down arrows located to the right of the display to adjust the cooking time between 1 and 12 hours in 15-minute increments.

4. Press START/STOP to initiate the cooking process.

5. When the cooking time reaches zero, the unit will beep and display "End" to indicate the end of the cooking session.

Sear/Sauté:

1. Before getting started with your cooking, be sure to remove the Crisper Tray from the pot and add your ingredients.

2. Next, move the SmartSwitch to AIR FRY/STOVETOP and use the center front arrows to select the desired heat setting, ranging from "Lo1" to "Hi5".

3. Press START/STOP to begin cooking, and the timer will start counting up. To turn off the SEAR/SAUTÉ function, press START/STOP. If you wish to switch to a different cooking function, press START/STOP to end the current cooking function, then use the SmartSwitch and center front arrows to select your desired Function.

Sous Vide

1. Before getting started, remove the crisper tray from the pot and add 12 cups of room-temperature water (referencing the marking on the inside).

2. To begin the sous vide process, close the lid and adjust the dial to AIR FRY/STOVETOP, then use the center arrows to select SOUS VIDE. The default temperature setting will be displayed. Utilize the up and down arrows to the left of the display to choose a temperature in 5-degree increments ranging between 120°F and 190°F.

3. The cook time will default to 3 hours. You can adjust the cooking time in 15-minute increments up to 12 hours, then 1-hour increments from 12 hours to 24 hours using the up and down arrows to the right of the display.

4. Press START/STOP to begin preheating. The unit will beep when preheating is complete, indicating that "ADD FOOD" will show on display. To place the bags in the water, use the water displacement method: Working with one bag at a time, leave a corner of the bag unzipped—as you slowly lower the bag into the water, the pressure of the water will force the bag open, allowing it to submerge.

Slow Cook

1. Before you get started with your slow cooker, make sure to remove the crisper tray and add your ingredients to the bottom of the pot. Don't forget to check the maximum fill line (indicated on the inside of the pot) to ensure you don't overfill.

2. Once you've done this, move the SmartSwitch to AIR FRY/STOVETOP, and then use the center front arrows to select SLOW COOK. The default temperature setting will now be displayed. Use the up and down arrows to the left of the display to select "Hi," "Lo," or "bUFFEt."

3. Next, use the up and down arrows to the right of the display to adjust the cooking time. When you're ready, press START/STOP to begin cooking.

4. Once the cooking time reaches zero, the unit will beep, automatically switch to Keep Warm mode, and start to count up.

4-Week Meal Plan

Week 1

Day 1:
Breakfast: Bacon & Eggs in Avocado
Lunch: Cauliflower & Chickpea Salad
Snack: Spicy Olives
Dinner: Spanish Chicken & Peppers
Dessert: Egg Nut Bars

Day 2:
Breakfast: Double-Dipped Cinnamon Biscuits
Lunch: Green Beans with Sun-Dried Tomatoes
Snack: Fried Pickles with Dressing
Dinner: Lebanese Malfouf
Dessert: Orange Muffins with Poppy Seeds

Day 3:
Breakfast: Meritage Large Eggs
Lunch: Mozzarella Bell Pepper Salad
Snack: Buffalo Cauliflower Wings
Dinner: Turkey Burgers with Potato Fries
Dessert: Zucchini Bread

Day 4:
Breakfast: Ham Omelet
Lunch: Cheese Zucchini Rice Fritters
Snack: Zucchini Chips
Dinner: Prosciutto-Wrapped Chicken with Squash
Dessert: Simple Lemon Pie

Day 5:
Breakfast: Easy Bacon Slices
Lunch: Zucchini Cubes with Mediterranean Dill Sauce
Snack: Lemon Mushrooms
Dinner: Lamb Kofta with Yogurt Sauce
Dessert: Cream Scones

Day 6:
Breakfast: Valerie's Sammies
Lunch: Wonderful Avocado Fries
Snack: Spicy Pecans
Dinner: Steak with Onion Gravy
Dessert: Amaretto Poached Pears

Day 7:
Breakfast: Spiced Veggie Frittata
Lunch: Cheese Stuffed Zucchini
Snack: Brussels Sprouts with Bacon
Dinner: Butter Turkey Breast
Dessert: Filled Apple Pies

Week 2

Day 1:
Breakfast: Bacon Spinach Muffins
Lunch: Halloumi Rainbow Omelet
Snack: Jalapeño Poppers Wrapped in Bacon
Dinner: Beef Tips with Onions
Dessert: Smith Apple Wedges

Day 2:
Breakfast: Sausage Patties
Lunch: Hearty Celery Croquettes
Snack: Seasoned Kale Chips
Dinner: Cilantro Butter Mahi Mahi
Dessert: Easy-Baked Apples

Day 3:
Breakfast: Buffalo Chicken Muffins
Lunch: Colby Cauliflower Fritters
Snack: Crispy Brussels Sprout Pieces
Dinner: Boneless Chicken Thighs
Dessert: Butter Banana Bread Pudding

Day 4:
Breakfast: Radish Fries
Lunch: Broccoli with Garlic Sauce
Snack: Corn Salsa
Dinner: Turkey Breast Tenderloin
Dessert: Filled Cherry-Berry Crisp

Day 5:
Breakfast: Typical Egg Sandwich
Lunch: Veggie Fritters
Snack: Delicious Corn Fritters
Dinner: Spice-Rubbed Ribeye
Dessert: Yummy Chocolate Cake

Day 6:
Breakfast: Southwestern Taco
Lunch: Chinese Cabbage & Peppers Bake
Snack: Avocado & Black Bean Rolls
Dinner: Shrimp with Orange Sauce
Dessert: Blueberry Muffins

Day 7:
Breakfast: Feta Egg Spinach Bake
Lunch: Onion Mushroom Burgers
Snack: Crusted Avocado Wedges
Dinner: Pineapple Chicken
Dessert: Coconut Cake with Pineapple Topping

Week 3

Day 1:
Breakfast: Homemade Cornbread
Lunch: Cheese Eggplant Casserole
Snack: Blooming Onion with Sauce
Dinner: Crusted Pork Tenderloin with Potatoes
Dessert: Orange Dundee Cake

Day 2:
Breakfast: Crispy Coconut Chips
Lunch: Tofu Kebabs
Snack: Beet Chips
Dinner: Cod Piccata with Potatoes
Dessert: Delicious Gingerbread

Day 3:
Breakfast: Tofu Donut Bites
Lunch: Flavorful Tofu & Pineapple
Snack: Spiced Kale Chips
Dinner: Stuffed Chicken Breasts
Dessert: Apple Blueberry Crumble

Day 4:
Breakfast: English Muffin Sandwich
Lunch: Black Olives & Beans Tortillas
Snack: Sweet Potato Chips with Parsley
Dinner: Glazed Baby Back Ribs
Dessert: Original Cake for One

Day 5:
Breakfast: Potato Oat Muffins
Lunch: Spanish Rice Taquitos
Snack: Tomato Bruschetta
Dinner: Salmon with Tomatoes and Green Beans
Dessert: Simple Coco Whip

Day 6:
Breakfast: Blueberry Crepes
Lunch: Cheese Bowtie Pasta Bake
Snack: Mini Cheese Sandwiches
Dinner: Classic Chicken Kebab
Dessert: Orange Muffins with Poppy Seeds

Day 7:
Breakfast: Pecan Oatmeal Bars
Lunch: Cheese Black Bean Quesadillas
Snack: Russet Potato Skins
Dinner: Easy Pork Tenderloin
Dessert: Egg Nut Bars

Week 4

Day 1:
Breakfast: Butter Peanut Sticks
Lunch: Cauliflower Casserole
Snack: Buffalo Cauliflower Bites
Dinner: Flavorful Flounder au Gratin
Dessert: Simple Lemon Pie

Day 2:
Breakfast: Portabella Mushroom Strips
Lunch: Green Beans with Sun-Dried Tomatoes
Snack: Spicy Olives
Dinner: Spiced Chicken Shawarma
Dessert: Filled Apple Pies

Day 3:
Breakfast: Bacon & Eggs in Avocado
Lunch: Cheese Zucchini Rice Fritters
Snack: Buffalo Cauliflower Wings
Dinner: Savory Pork Shoulder
Dessert: Cream Scones

Day 4:
Breakfast: Double-Dipped Cinnamon Biscuits
Lunch: Wonderful Avocado Fries
Snack: Lemon Mushrooms
Dinner: Sea Bass with Root Vegetables
Dessert: Amaretto Poached Pears

Day 5:
Breakfast: Ham Omelet
Lunch: Mozzarella Bell Pepper Salad
Snack: Zucchini Chips
Dinner: Lemon Chicken Thighs
Dessert: Smith Apple Wedges

Day 6:
Breakfast: Easy Bacon Slices
Lunch: Hearty Celery Croquettes
Snack: Spicy Pecans
Dinner: Deconstructed Chicago Hot Dogs
Dessert: Butter Banana Bread Pudding

Day 7:
Breakfast: Spiced Veggie Frittata
Lunch: Broccoli with Garlic Sauce
Snack: Jalapeño Poppers Wrapped in Bacon
Dinner: Sea Bass with Root Vegetables
Dessert: Yummy Chocolate Cake

Chapter 1 Breakfast Recipes

Bacon & Eggs in Avocado	15	Crispy Coconut Chips	21
Meritage Large Eggs	15	Radish Fries	21
Egg Onion Pizza	16	English Muffin Sandwich	22
Ham Omelet	16	Potato Oat Muffins	22
Spiced Veggie Frittata	17	Pecan Oatmeal Bars	23
Bacon Spinach Muffins	17	Blueberry Crepes	23
Sausage Patties	18	Butter Peanut Sticks	24
Buffalo Chicken Muffins	18	Homemade Cornbread	24
Typical Egg Sandwich	19	Double-Dipped Cinnamon Biscuits	25
Southwestern Taco	19	Easy Bacon Slices	25
Tofu Donut Bites	20	Valerie's Sammies	26
Feta Egg Spinach Bake	20	Portabella Mushroom Strips	26

Bacon & Eggs in Avocado

Prep Time: 5 minutes | Cook Time: 17 minutes | Serves: 1

⋯⋯⋯⋯⋯⋯⋯⋯⋯⋯⋯⋯⋯⋯⋯⋯⋯⋯⋯⋯⋯

1 large egg
1 avocado, halved, peeled, and pitted
2 slices bacon
Fresh parsley, for serving (optional)
Sea salt flakes, for garnish (optional)

⋯⋯⋯⋯⋯⋯⋯⋯⋯⋯⋯⋯⋯⋯⋯⋯⋯⋯⋯⋯⋯

1. Fill a small bowl with cool water. 2. Place the Crisper Tray in the bottom position. 3. Add the egg to it and close the lid. Move SmartSwitch to AIR FRY/STOVETOP, set the cooking temperature to 320 degrees F and the cooking time to 6 minutes (Or you can cook the egg for 7 minutes for a cooked yolk). 4. Transfer the egg to the bowl of cool water and let sit for 2 minutes. Peel and set aside. 5. Carve out extra space in the center of the avocado halves until the cavities are big enough to fit the soft-boiled egg. 6. Place the soft-boiled egg in the center of one half of the avocado and replace the other half of the avocado on top, so the avocado appears whole on the outside. 7. Starting at one end of the avocado, wrap the bacon around the avocado to completely cover it. Use toothpicks to hold the bacon in place. 8. Air-fry the bacon-wrapped avocado at 320 degrees F for 10 minutes, flipping halfway through cooking. 9. Serve on a bed of fresh parsley, and you can sprinkle with salt flakes if desired.

Per Serving: Calories 605; Fat: 54.64g; Sodium: 329mg; Carbs: 17.94g; Fiber: 13.5g; Sugar: 1.94g; Protein: 16.82g

Meritage Large Eggs

Prep Time: 5 minutes | Cook Time: 8 minutes | Serves: 2

⋯⋯⋯⋯⋯⋯⋯⋯⋯⋯⋯⋯⋯⋯⋯⋯⋯⋯⋯⋯⋯

2 teaspoons unsalted butter (or coconut oil for dairy-free), for greasing the ramekins
4 large eggs
2 teaspoons chopped fresh thyme
½ teaspoon fine sea salt
¼ teaspoon ground black pepper
2 tablespoons heavy cream
3 tablespoons finely grated Parmesan cheese
Fresh thyme leaves, for garnish (optional)

⋯⋯⋯⋯⋯⋯⋯⋯⋯⋯⋯⋯⋯⋯⋯⋯⋯⋯⋯⋯⋯

1. Grease two 4-ounce ramekins with the butter. 2. Crack 2 eggs into each ramekin and divide the thyme, salt, and pepper between the ramekins. 3. Pour 1 tablespoon of the heavy cream into each ramekin. Sprinkle each ramekin with 1½ tablespoons of the Parmesan cheese. 4. Place the Crisper Tray in the bottom position. Place the ramekins on the tray and close the lid. Move SmartSwitch to AIR FRY/STOVETOP, and then use the center front arrows to select BAKE/ROAST. Set the cooking temperature to 400 degrees F and the cooking time to 8 minutes. 5. Garnish the dish with a sprinkle of ground black pepper and thyme leaves, if desired. Best served fresh.

Per Serving: Calories 249; Fat: 19.25g; Sodium: 741mg; Carbs: 3.41g; Fiber: 0.2g; Sugar: 0.9g; Protein: 8.14g

Egg Onion Pizza

Prep Time: 5 minutes | Cook Time: 8 minutes | Serves: 1

- 2 large eggs
- ¼ cup unsweetened, unflavored almond milk (or unflavored hemp milk for nut-free)
- ¼ teaspoon fine sea salt
- ⅛ teaspoon ground black pepper
- ¼ cup diced onions
- ¼ cup shredded Parmesan cheese (omit for dairy-free)
- 6 pepperoni slices (omit for vegetarian)
- ¼ teaspoon dried oregano leaves
- ¼ cup pizza sauce, warmed, for serving

1. Whisk the eggs with almond milk, salt, and pepper in a bowl. 2. Pour the mixture into a suitable greased pan, then stir in the onions and top with the cheese, (if using), pepperoni slices (if using), and oregano. 3. Place the Crisper Tray in the bottom position. Place the pan on the tray and close the lid. 4. Move SmartSwitch to AIR FRY/STOVETOP, and then use the center front arrows to select BAKE/ROAST. 5. Set the cooking temperature to 350 degrees F and the cooking time to 8 minutes. 6. Loosen the eggs from the sides of the pan with a spatula and place them on a serving plate. 7. Drizzle the pizza sauce on top. Best served fresh.

Per Serving: Calories 740; Fat: 57.16g; Sodium: 1748mg; Carbs: 24.87g; Fiber: 8.4g; Sugar: 8.22g; Protein: 37.35g

Ham Omelet

Prep Time: 5 minutes | Cook Time: 8 minutes | Serves: 1

- 2 large eggs
- ¼ cup unsweetened, unflavored almond milk
- ¼ teaspoon fine sea salt
- ⅛ teaspoon ground black pepper
- ¼ cup diced ham (omit for vegetarian)
- ¼ cup diced green and red bell peppers
- 2 tablespoons diced green onions, plus more for garnish
- ¼ cup shredded cheddar cheese (about 1 ounce) (omit for dairy-free)
- Quartered cherry tomatoes, for serving (optional)

1. Whisk the eggs, almond milk, salt, pepper, ham, bell peppers, and green onions in a small bowl. 2. Pour the mixture into a suitable greased pan and add the cheese on top (if using). 3. Place the Crisper Tray in the bottom position. Place the pan on the tray and close the lid. Move SmartSwitch to AIR FRY/STOVETOP, and then use the center front arrows to select BAKE/ROAST. Set the cooking temperature to 350 degrees F and the cooking time to 8 minutes. 4. Loosen the omelet from the sides of the pan with a spatula and place it on a serving plate. 5. Garnish with green onions and serve with cherry tomatoes, if desired.

Per Serving: Calories 346; Fat: 22.48g; Sodium: 1345mg; Carbs: 9.38g; Fiber: 0.7g; Sugar: 7.06g; Protein: 26.13g

Spiced Veggie Frittata

Prep Time: 7 minutes | Cook Time: 23 minutes | Serves: 2

Avocado oil spray
¼ cup diced red onion
¼ cup diced red bell pepper
¼ cup finely chopped broccoli
4 large eggs
3 ounces shredded sharp Cheddar cheese, divided
½ teaspoon dried thyme
Sea salt
Freshly ground black pepper

1. Spray a suitable pan well with oil. Put the onion, pepper, and broccoli in the pan. 2. Place the Crisper Tray in the bottom position. Place the pan on the tray and close the lid. 3. Move SmartSwitch to AIR FRY/STOVETOP, and then use the center front arrows to select BAKE/ROAST. Set the cooking temperature to 350 degrees F and the cooking time to 5 minutes. 4. Beat the eggs in a medium bowl. Stir in half of the cheese, and season with the thyme, salt, and pepper. 5. Add the eggs to the pan and top with the remaining cheese, and then BAKE them at 350 degrees F for 16 to 18 minutes. 6. Serve warm.

Per Serving: Calories 227; Fat: 13.34g; Sodium: 691mg; Carbs: 7.58g; Fiber: 0.5g; Sugar: 4.29g; Protein: 18.71g

Bacon Spinach Muffins

Prep Time: 7 minutes | Cook Time: 15 minutes | Serves: 6

6 large eggs
¼ cup heavy (whipping) cream
½ teaspoon sea salt
¼ teaspoon freshly ground black pepper
¼ teaspoon cayenne pepper (optional)
¾ cup frozen chopped spinach, thawed and drained
4 strips cooked bacon, crumbled
2 ounces shredded Cheddar cheese

1. In a large bowl, whisk together the eggs, heavy cream, salt, black pepper, and cayenne pepper (if using). 2. Divide the spinach and bacon among 6 silicone muffin cups; divide the egg mixture among the muffin cups and then top them with the cheese. 3. Place the Crisper Tray in the bottom position. Place the muffin cups on the tray and close the lid. 4. Move SmartSwitch to AIR FRY/STOVETOP, and then use the center front arrows to select BAKE/ROAST. Set the cooking temperature to 300 degrees F and the cooking time to 14 minutes. 5. Serve warm.

Per Serving: Calories 122; Fat: 8.56g; Sodium: 434mg; Carbs: 2.65g; Fiber: 0.7g; Sugar: 1.13g; Protein: 8.73g

Sausage Patties

Prep Time: 10 minutes | Cook Time: 10 minutes | Serves: 8

1 pound ground pork
1 tablespoon coconut aminos
2 teaspoons liquid smoke
1 teaspoon dried sage
1 teaspoon sea salt
½ teaspoon fennel seeds
½ teaspoon dried thyme
½ teaspoon freshly ground black pepper
¼ teaspoon cayenne pepper

1. Combine the pork, coconut aminos, liquid smoke, sage, salt, fennel seeds, thyme, black pepper, and cayenne pepper in a large bowl until the seasonings are fully incorporated. 2. Shape the mixture into 8 equal-size patties. Using your thumb, make a dent in the center of each patty. 3. Place the patties on a plate and cover with plastic wrap. Refrigerate the patties for at least 30 minutes. 4. Place the Crisper Tray in the bottom position. Add the patties to it and close the lid. 5. Move SmartSwitch to AIR FRY/STOVETOP, set the cooking temperature to 400 degrees F and the cooking time to 9 minutes. 6. Flip the patties halfway through cooking. 7. Serve warm.

Per Serving: Calories 170; Fat: 11.83g; Sodium: 334mg; Carbs: 0.33g; Fiber: 0.2g; Sugar: 0.06g; Protein: 14.63g

Buffalo Chicken Muffins

Prep Time: 7 minutes | Cook Time: 16 minutes | Serves: 10

6 ounces shredded cooked chicken
3 ounces blue cheese, crumbled
2 tablespoons unsalted butter, melted
⅓ cup Buffalo hot sauce, such as Frank's RedHot
1 teaspoon minced garlic
6 large eggs
Sea salt
Freshly ground black pepper
Avocado oil spray

1. Stir together the chicken, blue cheese, melted butter, hot sauce, and garlic in a large bowl. 2. In a medium bowl or large liquid measuring cup, beat the eggs. Season them with salt and pepper. 3. Spray 10 silicone muffin cups with oil. Divide the chicken mixture among the cups, and pour the egg mixture over top. 4. Place the Crisper Tray in the bottom position. Place the muffin cups on the tray and close the lid. 5. Move SmartSwitch to AIR FRY/STOVETOP, and then use the center front arrows to select BAKE/ROAST. Set the cooking temperature to 300 degrees F and the cooking time to 16 minutes. 6. You might need bake them in batches. 7. Serve warm.

Per Serving: Calories 168; Fat: 3.63g; Sodium: 93mg; Carbs: 31.51g; Fiber: 2.3g; Sugar: 17.77g; Protein: 3.62g

Typical Egg Sandwich

Prep Time: 10 Minutes | Cook Time: 15 Minutes | Serves: 1

Avocado oil spray
1 large egg
Sea salt
Freshly ground black pepper
2 tablespoons unsalted butter, at room temperature
2 slices keto-friendly bread
2 slices Cheddar cheese
¼ avocado, sliced
Hot sauce, for serving

1. Line a suitable cake pan with parchment paper. 2. Spray a 3½-inch egg ring with oil, and then place it in the prepared pan. 3. Crack an egg into the egg ring and then season with salt and pepper. 4. Place the Crisper Tray in the bottom position. Place the pan on the tray and close the lid. 5. Move SmartSwitch to AIR FRY/STOVETOP, and then use the center front arrows to select BAKE/ROAST. Set the cooking temperature to 300 degrees F and the cooking time to 8 minutes. 6. When cooked, remove out the egg ring. 7. Spread the butter on one side of each bread slice and place them in the pan. 8. BAKE the bread at 300 degrees F for 4 minutes until the butter is melted and the bread is lightly toasted. 9. Place the egg on one of the toasted bread slices, and top with the cheese slices. Cook them for about 2 minutes more until the cheese melts. 10. Top the dish with the avocado and hot sauce, place the second bread slice on top, and serve.

Per Serving: Calories 633; Fat: 47.91g; Sodium: 835mg; Carbs: 27g; Fiber: 5.1g; Sugar: 3.17g; Protein: 25.53g

Southwestern Taco

Prep Time: 10 minutes | Cook Time: 10 minutes | Serves: 1

1 large egg, beaten
½ cup shredded mozzarella cheese
1 tablespoon finely ground blanched almond flour
1 tablespoon canned chopped green chiles
1 teaspoon Taco Seasoning
½ teaspoon baking powder
2 strips cooked bacon, crumbled
¼ avocado, diced
2 tablespoons shredded Cheddar cheese
2 tablespoons sour cream
1 tablespoon salsa
Chopped fresh cilantro, for serving (optional)
Hot sauce, for serving (optional)

1. In a medium bowl, whisk together the egg, mozzarella cheese, almond flour, chiles, taco seasoning, and baking powder. 2. Line a suitable baking pan with parchment paper. Spread the egg-cheese mixture in an even layer in the prepared pan. 3. Place the Crisper Tray in the bottom position. Place the pan on the tray and close the lid. 4. Move SmartSwitch to AIR FRY/STOVETOP, and then use the center front arrows to select BAKE/ROAST. Set the cooking temperature to 400 degrees F and the cooking time to 9 minutes. 5. When cooked, remove out the dish and top with the bacon, avocado, Cheddar cheese, sour cream, and salsa. 6. Serve warm with cilantro and hot sauce (if using).

Per Serving: Calories 417; Fat: 26.12g; Sodium: 1320mg; Carbs: 18.33g; Fiber: 6.4g; Sugar: 4.94g; Protein: 30.61g

Tofu Donut Bites

Prep Time: 10 minutes | Cook Time: 10 minutes | Serves: 4

- 1 tablespoon Bob's Red Mill egg replacer
- 2 tablespoons water
- 1 cup all-purpose white flour
- 4 tablespoons coconut sugar, divided
- 1 teaspoon baking powder
- ¼ teaspoon baking soda
- ⅛ teaspoon salt
- 4 ounces soft silken tofu
- 1 teaspoon pure vanilla extract
- 1 tablespoon melted vegan butter
- Oil for misting or cooking spray

1. In a medium bowl, combine the egg replacer and water and stir. 2. In a large bowl, stir together the flour, 2 tablespoons of sugar, baking powder, baking soda, and salt. 3. Add the tofu and vanilla to the egg mixture. Break apart the tofu and blend until fairly smooth. Stir in the melted vegan butter. 4. Add the tofu mixture to the dry ingredients and mix well. The dough may feel dry and crumbly. 5. Use the back of a spoon to knead the dry crumbs into the mixture until you have stiff dough that clings together. 6. Divide the dough into 16 portions and shape them into balls. 7. Mist the bites with oil and sprinkle the tops with the remaining coconut sugar. 8. Place the Crisper Tray in the bottom position. Add half of the bites to it and close the lid. 9. Move SmartSwitch to AIR FRY/STOVETOP, set the cooking temperature to 390 degrees F and the cooking time to 5 minutes. 10. When cooked, the center should be done and the outside should be lightly browned. 11. Cook the remaining bites. 12. Serve warm.

Per Serving: Calories 205; Fat: 5.3g; Sodium: 189mg; Carbs: 33.21g; Fiber: 0.9g; Sugar: 8.26g; Protein: 5.72g

Feta Egg Spinach Bake

Prep Time: 10 minutes | Cook Time: 25 minutes | Serves: 2

- Avocado oil spray
- ⅓ cup diced red onion
- 1 cup frozen chopped spinach, thawed and drained
- 4 large eggs
- ¼ cup heavy (whipping) cream
- Sea salt
- Freshly ground black pepper
- ¼ teaspoon cayenne pepper
- ½ cup crumbled feta cheese
- ¼ cup shredded Parmesan cheese

1. Spray a suitable baking pan with oil and then add the onion to the pan. 2. Place the Crisper Tray in the bottom position. Place the pan on the tray and close the lid. 3. Move SmartSwitch to AIR FRY/STOVETOP, and then use the center front arrows to select BAKE/ROAST. Set the cooking temperature to 350 degrees F and the cooking time to 7 minutes. 4. Sprinkle the spinach over the onion. 5. In a medium bowl, beat the eggs, heavy cream, salt, black pepper, and cayenne. Pour this mixture over the vegetables and then top them with feta and Parmesan cheese. 6. BAKE the food at 350 degrees F for 16 to 18 minutes more until the eggs are set and lightly brown. 7. Serve warm.

Per Serving: Calories 344; Fat: 26.54g; Sodium: 727mg; Carbs: 10.11g; Fiber: 2.7g; Sugar: 349g; Protein: 17.65g

Crispy Coconut Chips

Prep Time: 10 minutes | Cook Time: 15 minutes | Serves: 4

Oil for misting or cooking spray
2 cups unsweetened, large coconut chips
2 tablespoons low-sodium soy sauce
5 teaspoons liquid smoke
1 tablespoon maple syrup

1. Spray a suitable baking pan lightly with oil or nonstick spray. 2. Place the coconut chips in the baking pan. 3. In a small bowl, mix the soy sauce, liquid smoke, and syrup. 4. Pour the liquid over the coconut chips and stir well to distribute. 5. Place the Crisper Tray in the bottom position. Place the pan on the tray and close the lid. 6. Move SmartSwitch to AIR FRY/STOVETOP, and then use the center front arrows to select BAKE/ROAST. Set the cooking temperature to 360 degrees F and the cooking time to 7 minutes. 7. Stir the food twice during baking. 8. Serve hot or spread the chips on a baking sheet to cool slightly. The chips will crisp as they cool.

Per Serving: Calories 159; Fat: 13.48g; Sodium: 264mg; Carbs: 9.86g; Fiber: 3.6g; Sugar: 5.55g; Protein: 1.98g

Radish Fries

Prep Time: 10 minutes | Cook Time: 16 minutes | Serves: 4

1½ cups coarsely chopped radishes
½ cup chopped onion
1 jalapeño, seeded and diced
1 teaspoon garlic powder
½ teaspoon smoked paprika
Sea salt
Freshly ground black pepper
1 tablespoon avocado oil
2 tablespoons chopped fresh cilantro or parsley, for garnish

1. Place the Crisper Tray in the bottom position; add the radishes, onion, jalapeño, garlic powder, and paprika, then season them with salt and pepper and toss them with the oil. 2. Close the lid. Move SmartSwitch to AIR FRY/STOVETOP, set the cooking temperature to 350 degrees F and the cooking time to 8 minutes. 3. When the cooking time is up, increase the temperature to 400°F, and then cook for another 8 minutes. 4. Garnish the dish with cilantro or parsley. Serve warm.

Per Serving: Calories 52; Fat: 3.64g; Sodium: 59mg; Carbs: 4.73g; Fiber: 1.3g; Sugar: 2.06g; Protein: 0.91g

English Muffin Sandwich

Prep Time: 15 minutes | Cook Time: 5 minutes | Serves: 4

1 medium red apple
4 whole English muffins
¾ cup Cheddar-style shreds
Ground cinnamon
¼ cup coarsely chopped walnuts
¼ cup dried cranberries

1. Quarter and core the apple and cut each quarter lengthwise into ¼-inch slices. 2. Split 2 of the English muffins and lay them cut-side up. 3. On each bottom half, place a heaping tablespoon of cheese shreds and a quarter of the apple slices, which will overlap slightly. Sprinkle them with cinnamon to taste. 4. On each top half, place 1 tablespoon of nuts and 1 tablespoon of cranberries. Top them with a heaping tablespoon of cheese. 5. Place the Crisper Tray in the bottom position. Add the halves to it and close the lid. 6. Move SmartSwitch to AIR FRY/STOVETOP, set the cooking temperature to 390 degrees F and the cooking time to 5 minutes. 7. The muffins should be crispy on the bottom when cooked. 8. Transfer them to a plate. Close each muffin and use a spatula to press the tops down firmly. 9. Enjoy.

Per Serving: Calories 282; Fat: 11.53g; Sodium: 383mg; Carbs: 36.25g; Fiber: 6g; Sugar: 12.29g; Protein: 12g

Potato Oat Muffins

Prep Time: 10 minutes | Cook Time: 10 minutes | Serves: 4

1¼ cups rolled oats
¼ cup oat bran
¼ teaspoon ground ginger
¼ teaspoon salt (optional)
¼ cup chopped pecans
½ cup mashed sweet potatoes
3 tablespoons molasses
Oil for misting or cooking spray

1. In a large bowl, stir together the oats, oat bran, ginger, salt, and pecans. 2. Add the sweet potatoes and molasses and stir until combined and stiff. 3. Spray 8 muffin cups lightly with oil or cooking spray. 4. Divide the mixture evenly among 8 muffin cups and pack them tightly. 5. Place the Crisper Tray in the bottom position. Place the muffin cups on the tray and close the lid. 6. Move SmartSwitch to AIR FRY/STOVETOP, and then use the center front arrows to select BAKE/ROAST. Set the cooking temperature to 360 degrees F and the cooking time to 8 minutes. 7. The tops should turn dark brown. You can bake them muffins in batches. 8. Serve warm.

Per Serving: Calories 175; Fat: 6.98g; Sodium: 153mg; Carbs: 35.98g; Fiber: 6.3g; Sugar: 11.97g; Protein: 6.79g

Pecan Oatmeal Bars

Prep Time: 5 minutes | Cook Time: 10 minutes | Serves: 4

1 cup oatmeal

Oil for misting or cooking spray

Shredded coconut, 1 coconut yields

1 cup finely chopped pecans

¼ cup maple syrup for serving

1. Prepare the oatmeal according to the package directions. 2. While the oatmeal is still warm, pour it into a suitable baking pan. 3. Chill several hours or overnight, until the oatmeal feels cold and firm. 4. When ready to cook, cut the oatmeal into 3-inch to 4-inch squares. 5. Cut each square in half to make rectangles or triangles. 6. Mist the bottoms of the oatmeal slices with oil or cooking spray. 7. Sprinkle the tops lightly with coconut and chopped pecans, pressing them in gently, then spray the tops with oil. 8. Place the Crisper Tray in the bottom position. Add the slices to it and close the lid. 9. Move SmartSwitch to AIR FRY/STOVETOP, set the cooking temperature to 390 degrees F and the cooking time to 9 minutes. 10. The tops should turn brown and crispy when cooked. 11. Transfer the bars to serving plates. If any toppings fall off during cooking, sprinkle them over the bars and serve them hot with maple syrup. 12. Enjoy.

Per Serving: Calories 299; Fat: 20.38g; Sodium: 123mg; Carbs: 29.13g; Fiber: 4.2g; Sugar: 17.72g; Protein: 4.18g

Blueberry Crepes

Prep Time: 10 minutes | Cook Time: 5 minutes | Serves: 4

¼ cup soft silken tofu, drained (about 2 ounces)

3 tablespoons cream cheese

1 teaspoon grated lemon zest

½ teaspoon lemon juice

1½ teaspoons coconut sugar

½ cup fresh blueberries

4 (8-inch) flour tortillas

1. In a food processor, combine the tofu, cream cheese, lemon zest, lemon juice, and sugar and process until smooth. 2. Place 1 tablespoon of filling on each tortilla and spread evenly to within ½-inch of the edges. 3. Top each tortilla with 2 tablespoons of blueberries, placing them in a line close to one edge. Roll up. 4. Place the Crisper Tray in the bottom position. 5. Add the tortillas to it and close the lid. Move SmartSwitch to AIR FRY/STOVETOP, set the cooking temperature to 390 degrees F and the cooking time to 4 minutes. 6. You can cook them in batches. 7. The outside of the crepes should be lightly brown. 8. Serve warm.

Per Serving: Calories 195; Fat: 6.61g; Sodium: 384mg; Carbs: 28.49g; Fiber: 1.7g; Sugar: 4.89g; Protein: 5.68g

Butter Peanut Sticks

Prep Time: 10 minutes | Cook Time: 7 minutes | Serves: 4

2 tablespoons Bob's Red Mill egg replacer
¼ cup water
½ cup crushed cornflake crumbs
Day-old French bread or baguette loaf
6 tablespoons almond milk
1 teaspoon pure vanilla extract
½ teaspoon cinnamon
2 teaspoons coconut sugar
Oil for misting or cooking spray
½ cup peanut butter
2 large bananas, sliced

1. In a shallow dish, mix together the egg replacer and water; add the almond milk, vanilla, cinnamon, and sugar, and then stir them well. 2. Place the cornflake crumbs in another shallow dish. 3. Cut the bread into "sticks" of appropriate size. 4. Dip the bread sticks into the egg mixture, shake off the excess, and then roll them in the crumbs and mist with oil or cooking spray. 5. Place the Crisper Tray in the bottom position. Add the sticks to it and close the lid. 6. Move SmartSwitch to AIR FRY/STOVETOP, set the cooking temperature to 390 degrees F and the cooking time to 4 minutes. 7. The sticks should be brown and crispy when cooked. Transfer them to the serving plates. 8. Place the peanut butter in a suitable baking pan, and BAKE the butter at 390 degrees F for 2 minutes, stirring halfway through. 9. Top each serving of breakfast sticks with sliced bananas and a generous drizzle of warm peanut butter. Enjoy.

Per Serving: Calories 254; Fat: 9.28g; Sodium: 649mg; Carbs: 36.97g; Fiber: 3.5g; Sugar: 19.07g; Protein: 7.16g

Homemade Cornbread

Prep Time: 15 minutes | Cook Time: 26 minutes | Serves: 4

1 tablespoon flaxseed meal
2 tablespoons water
½ cup pecans, roughly chopped
½ cup white cornmeal
½ cup all-purpose white flour
2 teaspoons baking powder
½ teaspoon salt
2 tablespoons vegetable oil
½ cup almond milk
2 tablespoons molasses
Maple syrup for serving

1. Mix the flaxseed meal and water in a medium bowl and set aside. 2. Place the Crisper Tray in the bottom position. Add the pecans to it and close the lid. 3. Move SmartSwitch to AIR FRY/STOVETOP, set the cooking temperature to 360 degrees F and the cooking time to 3 minutes. Set aside. 4. Stir the cornmeal, flour, baking powder, and salt in a large bowl. 5. To the flaxseed mixture, add the oil, milk, and molasses and whisk together. 6. Pour the wet ingredients into the dry ingredients and stir to mix well. 7. Pour the batter into a suitable baking pan. 8. Place the Crisper Tray in the bottom position. Place the pan on the tray and close the lid. 9. Move SmartSwitch to AIR FRY/STOVETOP, and then use the center front arrows to select BAKE/ROAST. Set the cooking temperature to 360 degrees F and the cooking time to 13 minutes. 10. Let the food cool for about 5 minutes after baking. 11. Cut the bread diagonally into 4 wedges. Top each wedges with the toasted pecans and maple syrup. 12. Enjoy.

Per Serving: Calories 318; Fat: 17.89g; Sodium: 325mg; Carbs: 37.57g; Fiber: 3.6g; Sugar: 10.77g; Protein: 4.65g

Double-Dipped Cinnamon Biscuits

Prep Time: 15 minutes | Cook Time: 15 minutes | Serves: 4

- 2 cups blanched almond flour
- ½ cup Swerve confectioners'-style sweetener or equivalent amount of liquid or powdered sweetener
- 1 teaspoon baking powder
- ½ teaspoon fine sea salt
- ¼ cup plus 2 tablespoons (¾ stick) very cold unsalted butter
- ¼ cup unsweetened, unflavored almond milk
- 1 large egg
- 1 teaspoon vanilla extract
- 3 teaspoons ground cinnamon

Glaze:

- ½ cup Swerve confectioners'-style sweetener or equivalent amount of powdered sweetener
- ¼ cup heavy cream or unsweetened, unflavored almond milk

1. Mix together the almond flour, sweetener, baking powder, and salt in a medium bowl. Cut the butter into ½-inch squares, and then use a hand mixer to work the butter into the dry ingredients. The mixture should have chunks of butter. 2. Whisk the almond milk, egg, and vanilla extract in a small bowl until blended. 3. Stir the wet ingredients into the dry ingredients with a fork until large clumps form; add the cinnamon and swirl into the dough. 4. Form the dough into sixteen 1-inch balls. 5. Place the Crisper Tray in the bottom position. Place the balls on the tray with spacing them about ½ inch apart and close the lid. 6. Move SmartSwitch to AIR FRY/STOVETOP, and then use the center front arrows to select BAKE/ROAST. Set the cooking temperature to 350 degrees F and the cooking time to 13 minutes. 7. Place the powdered sweetener in a small bowl and slowly stir in the heavy cream with a fork. 8. When the biscuits have cooled somewhat, dip the tops into the glaze, allow it to dry a bit, and then dip again for a thick glaze. 9. Serve warm or at room temperature.

Per Serving: Calories 222; Fat: 12.14g; Sodium: 479mg; Carbs: 29.69g; Fiber: 1.6g; Sugar: 24.46g; Protein: 1.45g

Easy Bacon Slices

Prep Time: 5 minutes | Cook Time: 6 minutes | Serves: 2

4 slices thin-cut bacon or beef bacon

1. Place the Crisper Tray in the bottom position. 2. Add the bacon to it in a single layer and close the lid. 3. Move SmartSwitch to AIR FRY/STOVETOP, set the cooking temperature to 360 degrees F and the cooking time to 6 minutes. 4. Check the bacon after 4 minutes to make sure it is not overcooking. 5. Best served fresh. 6. You can store the extras in an airtight container in the fridge for up to 4 days, and reheat them at 360 degrees F for 2 minutes.

Per Serving: Calories 212; Fat: 20.42g; Sodium: 244mg; Carbs: 0.43g; Fiber: 0g; Sugar: 0.43g; Protein: 6.52g

Valerie's Sammies

Prep Time: 15 minutes | Cook Time: 20 minutes | Serves: 5

Biscuits:

6 large egg whites

2 cups blanched almond flour, plus more if needed

1½ teaspoons baking powder

½ teaspoon fine sea salt

¼ cup (½ stick) very cold unsalted butter (or lard for dairy-free), cut into ¼-inch pieces

Eggs:

5 large eggs

½ teaspoon fine sea salt

¼ teaspoon ground black pepper

5 (1-ounce) slices cheddar cheese (omit for dairy-free)

10 thin slices ham

1. Grease two suitable pie pans or two baking pans. 2. In a medium-sized bowl, whip the egg whites with a hand mixer until very stiff. Set aside. 3. In a separate medium-sized bowl, stir together the almond flour, baking powder, and salt until well combined. Cut in the butter. 4. Gently fold the flour mixture into the egg whites with a rubber spatula. If the dough is too wet to form into mounds, add a few tablespoons of almond flour until the dough holds together well. 5. Divide the dough into 5 equal portions and drop them about 1-inch apart on one of the greased pie pans. 6. Place the Crisper Tray in the bottom position. Place the pan on the tray and close the lid. 7. Move SmartSwitch to AIR FRY/STOVETOP, and then use the center front arrows to select BAKE/ROAST. Set the cooking temperature to 350 degrees F and the cooking time to 14 minutes. 8. Cook the biscuit in batches. When cooked, the biscuits should be golden brown. Set aside. 9. Crack the eggs into the remaining greased pie pan and sprinkle with the salt and pepper. 10. Bake the eggs at 375 degrees F for 5 minutes or until they are cooked to your liking. 11. Top each egg yolk with a slice of cheese (if using), and cook them for another minute, or until the cheese is melted. 12. Once the biscuits are cool, slice them in half lengthwise. Place 1 cooked egg topped with cheese and 2 slices of ham in each biscuit. 13. Store leftover biscuits, eggs, and ham in separate airtight containers in the fridge for up to 3 days. Reheat the biscuits and eggs at 350 degrees F air fryer for about 5 minutes.

Per Serving: Calories 295; Fat: 21.99g; Sodium: 1359mg; Carbs: 2.74g; Fiber: 0.1g; Sugar: 0.6g; Protein: 21.73g

Portabella Mushroom Strips

Prep Time: 15 minutes | Cook Time: 7 minutes | Serves: 2

2 large portabella mushrooms, stems removed

1 teaspoon smoked

paprika

2 teaspoons maple syrup

⅛ teaspoon salt

2 tablespoons oil

1. Clean the portabellas and scrape out the gills with the tip of a knife. 2. Slice ¼-inch thick and spread the slices on a cutting board. 3. In a small bowl, mix together the smoked paprika, maple syrup, salt, and oil. 4. Brush the seasoned oil on both sides of the mushroom slices. 5. Place the Crisper Tray in the bottom position. Add the mushroom slices to it in a single layer and close the lid. 6. Move SmartSwitch to AIR FRY/STOVETOP, set the cooking temperature to 390 degrees F and the cooking time to 7 minutes. 7. Serve.

Per Serving: Calories 159; Fat: 14.05g; Sodium: 164mg; Carbs: 8.26g; Fiber: 1.5g; Sugar: 6.18g; Protein: 1.94g

Chapter 2 Vegetable and Sides Recipes

Cauliflower & Chickpea Salad 28

Green Beans with Sun-Dried Tomatoes ...28

Mozzarella Bell Pepper Salad...............29

Cheese Zucchini Rice Fritters...............29

Wonderful Avocado Fries 30

Zucchini Cubes with Mediterranean Dill Sauce 30

Cheese Stuffed Zucchini 31

Halloumi Rainbow Omelet 31

Hearty Celery Croquettes 32

Colby Cauliflower Fritters 32

Broccoli with Garlic Sauce 33

Veggie Fritters 33

Chinese Cabbage & Peppers Bake 34

Onion Mushroom Burgers 34

Tofu Kebabs 35

Flavorful Tofu & Pineapple 35

Cheese Eggplant Casserole.................36

Black Olives & Beans Tortillas 36

Cheese Bowtie Pasta Bake 37

Cheese Black Bean Quesadillas 37

Cauliflower Casserole.......................38

Spanish Rice Taquitos.......................38

Cauliflower & Chickpea Salad

Prep Time: 20 minutes | Cook Time: 23 minutes | Serves: 4

- 3½ tablespoons extra-virgin olive oil
- 1½ teaspoons curry powder
- Salt and pepper
- 1 head cauliflower (2 pounds), cored and cut into 1½-inch florets
- ¼ cup plain yogurt
- 2 tablespoons chopped fresh cilantro
- 1½ teaspoons lime juice
- 1 garlic clove, minced
- 1 (15-ounce) can chickpeas, rinsed
- 3 ounces seedless red grapes, halved (½ cup)
- ¼ cup roasted cashews, chopped

1 Whisk 1½ tablespoons oil, curry powder, ⅛ teaspoon salt, and ⅛ teaspoon pepper together in medium bowl. Add cauliflower and toss to coat; transfer to air-fryer basket. Place basket in air fryer and set temperature to 400 degrees. Cook cauliflower until tender and golden at edges, 23 to 25 minutes, tossing halfway through cooking. 2 Set cauliflower aside to cool slightly. Meanwhile, whisk yogurt, 1 tablespoon cilantro, lime juice, garlic, ⅛ teaspoon salt, ⅛ teaspoon pepper, and remaining 2 tablespoons oil together in serving bowl. Add cooled cauliflower and chickpeas and toss to coat. Season with salt and pepper to taste. Sprinkle with grapes, cashews, and remaining 1 tablespoon cilantro. Serve.

Per Serving: Calories 282; Fat: 16.25g; Sodium: 379mg; Carbs: 28.92g; Fiber: 6.7g; Sugar: 10.13g; Protein: 8.75g

Green Beans with Sun-Dried Tomatoes

Prep Time: 15 minutes | Cook Time: 15 minutes | Serves: 4

- 1 pound green beans, trimmed and halved
- 2 teaspoons extra-virgin olive oil
- Salt and pepper
- ½ cup torn fresh basil
- ⅓ cup oil-packed sun-dried tomatoes, rinsed, patted dry, and chopped
- 1 tablespoon lemon juice
- 2 ounces goat cheese, crumbled (½ cup)
- ¼ cup roasted sunflower seeds

1. Toss green beans with 1 teaspoon oil, ⅛ teaspoon salt, and ⅛ teaspoon pepper in bowl. 2. Place the Crisper Tray in the bottom position. Place the green beans on the tray and close the lid. 3. Move SmartSwitch to AIR FRY/STOVETOP, and then use the center front arrows to select BAKE/ROAST. Set the cooking temperature to 400 degrees F and the cooking time to 15 minutes. 4. Toss the roasted green beans with remaining 1 teaspoon oil, basil, sun-dried tomatoes, and lemon juice in large bowl. Season them with salt and pepper to taste. 5. Transfer them to serving dish and sprinkle with goat cheese and sunflower seeds. Enjoy.

Per Serving: Calories 282; Fat: 16.25g; Sodium: 379mg; Carbs: 28.92g; Fiber: 6.7g; Sugar: 10.13g; Protein: 8.75g

Mozzarella Bell Pepper Salad

Prep Time: 35 minutes | Cook Time: 25 minutes | Serves: 2

....

4 small bell peppers (red, orange, and/or yellow)
2 tablespoons extra-virgin olive oil
1 tablespoon balsamic vinegar
1 garlic clove, minced
Salt and pepper
2 ounces fresh mozzarella cheese, torn into 1-inch pieces
2 tablespoons torn fresh basil
1 tablespoon pine nuts, toasted

....

1. Trim ½ inch from top and bottom of bell peppers. 2. Using paring knife, remove ribs, core, and seeds and discard. 3. Place the Crisper Tray in the bottom position. Place the bell peppers on the tray and close the lid. 4. Move SmartSwitch to AIR FRY/STOVETOP, and then use the center front arrows to select BAKE/ROAST. Set the cooking temperature to 400 degrees F and the cooking time to 25 minutes. 5. Flip the bell peppers halfway through. 6. Transfer bell peppers to bowl, cover tightly with plastic wrap, and let steam for 10 minutes. 7. Whisk oil, vinegar, garlic, ⅛ teaspoon salt, and ⅛ teaspoon pepper together in serving dish. 8. Uncover bowl to let bell peppers cool slightly. 9. When cool enough to handle, peel bell peppers and discard skin, then cut bell peppers into 1-inch-wide strips. 10. Add bell peppers and mozzarella to bowl with dressing and toss to coat; season them with salt and pepper to taste. 11. Sprinkle the dish with basil and pine nuts. Enjoy.

Per Serving: Calories 160; Fat: 6.61g; Sodium: 426mg; Carbs: 14.09g; Fiber: 4.1g; Sugar: 9.46g; Protein: 11.08g

Cheese Zucchini Rice Fritters

Prep Time: 20 minutes | Cook Time: 15 minutes | Serves: 4

....

3 cups (495 g) cooked rice
2 cups (240 g) grated cheese, such as Cheddar, Swiss, or Gruyère
1 medium zucchini, grated (about 2 cups)
4 scallions, white and light green parts only, sliced
¼ cup (24 g) tightly packed chopped fresh mint
3 eggs, beaten
Kosher salt and pepper to taste
1¼ cups (83 g) panko bread crumbs
Vegetable oil for spraying
Lemon wedges for serving

....

1. Combine the cooked rice, grated cheese, grated zucchini, scallions, and mint in a large bowl; add the beaten eggs and season with salt and pepper, stir them to combine well, making sure the egg is evenly distributed through the rice. 2. Spread the panko on a plate. Scoop out approximately ½ cup of the rice mixture and form into a ball with your hands, pressing firmly to make the fritters as tight and well-packed as possible. 3. Dredge the ball in the panko. Repeat with the remaining rice mixture. 4. You should be able to make 8 or 9 fritters. 5. Place half the fritters on a plate and chill until needed. 6. Place the Crisper Tray in the bottom position. Add the fritters to it, spray them with oil, and close the lid. 7. Move SmartSwitch to AIR FRY/STOVETOP, set the cooking temperature to 400 degrees F and the cooking time to 12 minutes. 8. You can cook the fritters in batches. 9. Serve the rice fritters with lemon wedges for spritzing.

Per Serving: Calories 685; Fat: 47.21g; Sodium: 540mg; Carbs: 53.68g; Fiber: 19.5g; Sugar: 3.46g; Protein: 38.8g

Wonderful Avocado Fries

Prep Time: 20 minutes | Cook Time: 30 minutes | Serves: 4

½ head garlic (6-7 cloves)
½ cup almond meal
Sea salt and ground black pepper, to taste
2 eggs
½ cup parmesan cheese, grated
2 avocados, cut into wedges

Sauce:
½ cup mayonnaise
1 teaspoon lemon juice
1 teaspoon mustard

1. Place the garlic on a piece of aluminum foil and spritz with cooking spray. Wrap the garlic in the foil. 2. AIR-FRY the garlic in the Ninja S peedi Rapid Cooker & Air Fryer at 400 degrees F for 12 minutes. 3. Check the garlic, open the top of the foil and continue to cook for 10 minutes more. 4. Let the garlic cool for 10 to 15 minutes; remove the cloves by squeezing them out of the skins; mash the garlic and reserve. 5. In a shallow bowl, combine the almond meal, salt, and black pepper. In another shallow dish, whisk the eggs until frothy. 6. Place the parmesan cheese in a third shallow dish. 7. Dredge the avocado wedges in the almond meal mixture, shaking off the excess. Then, dip in the egg mixture; lastly, dredge in parmesan cheese. 8. Spritz the avocado wedges with cooking oil on all sides. 9. AIR-FRY the avocado wedges at 395 degrees F for 8 minutes, turning them halfway through. 10. Combine the sauce ingredients with the smashed roasted garlic in a clean bowl. 11. To serve, divide the avocado fries between plates and top with the sauce. Enjoy!

Per Serving: Calories 369; Fat: 32.74g; Sodium: 531mg; Carbs: 14.73g; Fiber: 7.4g; Sugar: 1.93g; Protein: 12.47g

Zucchini Cubes with Mediterranean Dill Sauce

Prep Time: 4 minutes | Cook Time: 20 minutes | Serves: 4

1 pound zucchini, peeled and cubed
2 tablespoons melted butter
1 teaspoon sea salt flakes
1 sprig rosemary, leaves only, crushed
2 sprigs thyme, leaves only, crushed
½ teaspoon freshly cracked black peppercorns

For Mediterranean Dipping Sauce:
½ cup mascarpone cheese
⅓ cup yogurt
1 tablespoon fresh dill, chopped
1 tablespoon olive oil

1. Soak the potato cubes in a bowl with cold water for about 35 minutes. 2. Dry the soaked potato cubes using a paper towel. 3. Thoroughly whisk the melted butter with sea salt flakes, rosemary, thyme, and freshly cracked peppercorns in a mixing dish. 4. Rub the potato cubes with this spice mix. 5. Place the Crisper Tray in the bottom position. Add the potato cubes to it and close the lid. 6. Move SmartSwitch to AIR FRY/STOVETOP, set the cooking temperature to 350 degrees F and the cooking time to 20 minutes. 7. At the same time, mix the remaining ingredients to make the dipping sauce. 8. Serve warm potatoes with Mediterranean sauce.

Per Serving: Calories 168; Fat: 14.13g; Sodium: 755mg; Carbs: 5.92g; Fiber: 1.6g; Sugar: 1.32g; Protein: 6.87g

Cheese Stuffed Zucchini

Prep Time: 10 minutes | Cook Time: 8 minutes | Serves: 4

....

1 large zucchini, cut into four pieces
2 tablespoons olive oil
1 cup Ricotta cheese, room temperature
2 tablespoons scallions, chopped
1 heaping tablespoon fresh parsley, roughly chopped
1 heaping tablespoon coriander, minced
2 ounces Cheddar cheese, preferably freshly grated
1 teaspoon celery seeds
½ teaspoon salt
½ teaspoon garlic pepper

....

1. Place the Crisper Tray in the bottom position. Place the zucchini on the tray and close the lid. 2. Move SmartSwitch to AIR FRY/STOVETOP, and then use the center front arrows to select BAKE/ROAST. Set the cooking temperature to 350 degrees F and the cooking time to 10 minutes. 3. Check for doneness and cook for 2-3 minutes longer if needed. 4. Mix all of the remaining ingredients. 5. Divide the stuffing among all zucchini pieces and bake for an additional 5 minutes. 6. Serve warm.

Per Serving: Calories 199; Fat: 16.22g; Sodium: 502mg; Carbs: 4.56g; Fiber: 0.3g; Sugar: 1.54g; Protein: 9.28g

Halloumi Rainbow Omelet

Prep Time: 5 minutes | Cook Time: 13 minutes | Serves: 2

....

3 tablespoons plain milk
4 eggs, whisked
1 teaspoon melted butter
Kosher salt and freshly ground black pepper, to taste
1 red bell pepper, deveined and chopped
1 yellow bell pepper, deveined and chopped
1 white onion, finely chopped
½ cup baby spinach leaves, roughly chopped
½ cup Halloumi cheese, shaved

....

1. Stir all of the ingredients in a suitable baking pan. 2. Place the Crisper Tray in the bottom position. Place the pan on the tray and close the lid. 3. Move SmartSwitch to AIR FRY/STOVETOP, and then use the center front arrows to select BAKE/ROAST. Set the cooking temperature to 350 degrees F and the cooking time to 13 minutes. 4. Serve warm.

Per Serving: Calories 448; Fat: 29.76g; Sodium: 493mg; Carbs: 18.65g; Fiber: 3.2g; Sugar: 6.93g; Protein: 27.55g

Hearty Celery Croquettes

Prep Time: 10 minutes | Cook Time: 6 minutes | Serves: 4

2 medium-sized celery stalks, trimmed and grated
½ cup of leek, finely chopped
1 tablespoon garlic paste
¼ teaspoon freshly cracked black pepper
1 teaspoon fine sea salt
1 tablespoon fresh dill, finely chopped
1 egg, lightly whisked
¼ cup almond flour
½ cup parmesan cheese, freshly grated
¼ teaspoon baking powder
2 tablespoons fresh chives, chopped
4 tablespoons mayonnaise

1. Place the celery on a paper towel and squeeze them to remove excess liquid. 2. Combine the vegetables with the other ingredients, except the chives and mayo. 3. Shape the balls using 1 tablespoon of the vegetable mixture. Gently flatten each ball with your palm or a wide spatula. 4. Spritz the croquettes with non-stick cooking oil. 5. Place the Crisper Tray in the bottom position. Add the croquettes to it and close the lid. Move SmartSwitch to AIR FRY/STOVETOP, set the cooking temperature to 360 degrees F and the cooking time to 6 minutes. 6. Mix fresh chives and mayonnaise. Serve warm croquettes with chive mayo. Bon appétit!

Per Serving: Calories 152; Fat: 11.01g; Sodium: 959mg; Carbs: 6.39g; Fiber: 1g; Sugar: 1.04g; Protein: 7.43g

Colby Cauliflower Fritters

Prep Time: 5 minutes | Cook Time: 10 minutes | Serves: 8

2 pounds cauliflower florets
½ cup scallions, finely chopped
½ teaspoon freshly ground black pepper, or more to taste
1 tablespoon fine sea salt
½ teaspoon hot paprika
2 cups Colby cheese, shredded
1 cup parmesan cheese, grated
¼ cup canola oil

1. Boil the cauliflower until fork tender. Drain, peel and mash your cauliflower. 2. Thoroughly mix the mashed cauliflower with scallions, pepper, salt, paprika, and Colby cheese. Then, shape the balls using your hands. 3. Flatten the balls to make the patties. 4. Roll the patties over grated parmesan cheese. Drizzle canola oil over them. 5. Place the Crisper Tray in the bottom position. Add the food to it and close the lid. 6. Move SmartSwitch to AIR FRY/STOVETOP, set the cooking temperature to 360 degrees F and the cooking time to 10 minutes. 7. Serve with tabasco mayo if desired.

Per Serving: Calories 274; Fat: 21.24g; Sodium: 1332mg; Carbs: 8.76g; Fiber: 2.5g; Sugar: 2.51g; Protein: 13.71g

Broccoli with Garlic Sauce

Prep Time: 10 minutes | Cook Time: 7 minutes | Serves: 4

2 tablespoons vegetable oil of choice
Kosher salt and freshly ground black pepper, to taste
1 pound broccoli florets

For the Dipping Sauce:
2 teaspoons dried rosemary, crushed
3 garlic cloves, minced
⅓ teaspoon dried marjoram, crushed
¼ cup sour cream
⅓ cup mayonnaise

1. Lightly grease the broccoli with a thin layer of vegetable oil and season with salt and ground black pepper. 2. Place the Crisper Tray in the bottom position. Place the food on the tray and close the lid. 3. Move SmartSwitch to AIR FRY/STOVETOP, and then use the center front arrows to select BAKE/ROAST. Set the cooking temperature to 395 degrees F and the cooking time to 15 minutes. 4. Toss them once or twice during cooking. 5. Prepare the dipping sauce by mixing all the sauce ingredients. 6. Serve warm broccoli with the dipping sauce and enjoy!

Per Serving: Calories 172; Fat: 15.23g; Sodium: 203mg; Carbs: 6.07g; Fiber: 3.5g; Sugar: 0.66g; Protein: 5.5g

Veggie Fritters

Prep Time: 15 minutes | Cook Time: 15 minutes | Serves: 3

1 cup celery, chopped
1 cup cauliflower rice
2 garlic cloves, minced
1 shallot, chopped
Sea salt and ground black pepper, to taste
2 tablespoons fresh parsley, chopped
1 egg, well beaten
1 cup Romano cheese, grated
½ cup almond flour
1 tablespoon olive oil

1. Mix the veggies, spices, egg, almond flour, and Romano cheese until everything is well incorporated. 2. Take 1 tablespoon of the veggie mixture and roll into a ball. 3. Roll the balls onto the dried bread flakes. 4. Brush the veggie balls with olive oil on all sides. 5. Place the Crisper Tray in the bottom position. 6. Add the balls to it and close the lid. Move SmartSwitch to AIR FRY/STOVETOP, set the cooking temperature to 360 degrees F and the cooking time to 15 minutes. 7. The balls should be crispy when cooked. 8. Serve warm.

Per Serving: Calories 275; Fat: 21.36g; Sodium: 339mg; Carbs: 6.25g; Fiber: 1.7g; Sugar: 2.65g; Protein: 15.31g

Chinese Cabbage & Peppers Bake

Prep Time: 10 minutes | Cook Time: 30 minutes | Serves: 4

½ pound Chinese cabbage, roughly chopped
2 bell peppers, seeded and sliced
1 jalapeno pepper, seeded and sliced
1 onion, thickly sliced
2 garlic cloves, sliced
½ stick butter
4 tablespoons flaxseed meal
½ cup milk
1 cup cream cheese
Sea salt and freshly ground black pepper, to taste
½ teaspoon cayenne pepper
1 cup Monterey Jack cheese, shredded

1. Bring a pan of salted water to a boil. Boil the Chinese cabbage for 2 to 3 minutes. 2. Transfer the Chinese cabbage to cold water to stop the cooking process. 3. Place the Chinese cabbage in a lightly greased casserole dish, and then add the peppers, onion, and garlic. 4. Melt the butter in a saucepan over a moderate heat. Gradually add the flaxseed meal and cook for 2 minutes to form a paste. 5. Slowly pour in the milk, stirring continuously until a thick sauce forms. 6. Add the cream cheese, and season them with the salt, black pepper, and cayenne pepper. 7. Add the mixture to the casserole dish. 8. Top them with the shredded Monterey Jack cheese. 9. Place the Crisper Tray in the bottom position. Place the mold on the tray and close the lid. 10. Move SmartSwitch to AIR FRY/STOVETOP, and then use the center front arrows to select BAKE/ROAST. Set the cooking temperature to 390 degrees F and the cooking time to 25 minutes. 11. Serve hot.

Per Serving: Calories 404; Fat: 33.38g; Sodium: 488mg; Carbs: 12.15g; Fiber: 4.2g; Sugar: 6.19g; Protein: 16.59g

Onion Mushroom Burgers

Prep Time: 25 minutes | Cook Time: 8 minutes | Serves: 4

3 tbsp. balsamic vinegar
1 tbsp. reduced-sodium soy sauce
1 tsp. Dijon mustard
2 garlic cloves, minced
4 Portobello mushroom caps, stems removed and gills scooped out
4 vegan hamburger buns, toasted
½ cup hummus
1 red onion, sliced
1 avocado, sliced
Butter or green leaf lettuce

1. In a large bowl, whisk together the balsamic vinegar, soy sauce, mustard, and garlic. Brush the mushrooms with the sauce and allow marinating for 10 minutes. 2. Place the Crisper Tray in the bottom position. 3. Add the mushrooms to it and close the lid. 4. Move SmartSwitch to AIR FRY/STOVETOP, set the cooking temperature to 400 degrees F and the cooking time to 8 minutes. 5. Flip the mushrooms halfway through. 6. Allow the mushrooms to cool in the fryer basket for 2 to 3 minutes. 7. Slather the buns with the hummus and fill with an equal amount of the mushrooms, onion, avocado, and lettuce. 8. Serve immediately.

Per Serving: Calories 511; Fat: 26.48g; Sodium: 725mg; Carbs: 50.08g; Fiber: 7.3g; Sugar: 10.9g; Protein: 20.7g

Tofu Kebabs

Prep Time: 10 minutes | Cook Time: 10 minutes | Serves: 6

16 oz. (450g) extra-firm tofu, drained
2 red bell peppers, cut into 1½-inch (3.75cm) pieces
1 red onion, cut into 1½-inch (3.75cm) pieces
2 tbsp. reduced-sodium soy sauce

FOR THE SAUCE
3 tbsp. creamy peanut butter
2 tbsp. reduced-sodium soy sauce
2 tbsp. water
1 tbsp. rice vinegar
1 tsp. agave nectar
1 tsp. crushed garlic

1. Slice the tofu into 4 large, flat pieces. 2. Wrap the tofu in a towel and place a large pot on top of the towel for 15 minutes to help remove any excess water. 3. Cut the tofu into 1½-inch pieces. 4. Combine the tofu, peppers, onion, and soy sauce in a large bowl. 5. Thread the tofu, pepper, and onion pieces onto bamboo skewers in alternating order. 6. Place the Crisper Tray in the bottom position. 7. Add the food to it and close the lid. Move SmartSwitch to AIR FRY/STOVETOP, set the cooking temperature to 400 degrees F and the cooking time to 10 minutes. 8. When cooked, the vegetable should be tender and the tofu should be golden brown and crispy around the edges. 9. In a medium bowl, make the peanut sauce by whisking together the ingredients. 10. Transfer the kebabs to a platter and serve immediately with the peanut sauce.

Per Serving: Calories 137; Fat: 7.86g; Sodium: 289mg; Carbs: 9.35g; Fiber: 1.2g; Sugar: 5.55g; Protein: 9.31g

Flavorful Tofu & Pineapple

Prep Time: 15 minutes | Cook Time: 15 minutes | Serves: 4

2 tbsp. chili paste (sambal oelek recommended)
¼ cup water
2 tbsp. white vinegar
½ tsp. chopped garlic
¼ cup granulated sugar
½ tsp. kosher salt
14oz. (400g) extra-firm tofu
1 tbsp. cornstarch
1½ cups diced pineapple
4 cups cooked brown rice

1. In a blender, combine the chili paste, water, vinegar, garlic, sugar, and salt. Blend them until the sugar is dissolved. 2. Transfer the mixture to a small saucepan on the stovetop over medium heat. Bring to a simmer and cook for 10 minutes to thicken. Set aside. 3. Dice the tofu and remove the liquid by gently pressing with paper towels or a clean dish towel. 4. In a medium bowl, combine the tofu and cornstarch. 5. Place the Crisper Tray in the bottom position. Add the tofu to it and close the lid. 6. Move SmartSwitch to AIR FRY/STOVETOP, set the cooking temperature to 400 degrees F and the cooking time to 15 minutes. 7. After 10 minutes of cooking time, add pineapple to the pot. 8. When cooked, the tofu should be golden and crispy. 9. Transfer the mixture to a serving bowl. Add half the chili sauce and toss well to coat. 10. Serve immediately with the brown rice and the remaining sauce.

Per Serving: Calories 408; Fat: 8.19g; Sodium: 425mg; Carbs: 71.65g; Fiber: 6.1g; Sugar: 21.11g; Protein: 15.8g

Cheese Eggplant Casserole

Prep Time: 35 minutes | Cook Time: 25 minutes | Serves: 2

- 1 large eggplant, peeled and diced
- 1 tbsp. olive oil
- ½ tsp. dried oregano
- 1 tsp. kosher salt
- ¼ tsp. freshly ground black pepper
- 1½ cups marinara sauce
- ½ cup vegan ricotta-style cheese
- ¾ cup shredded vegan mozzarella-style cheese (Daiya recommended)
- 3 tbsp. panko breadcrumbs

1. In a large bowl, combine the eggplant, olive oil, oregano, salt, and pepper. 2. Place the Crisper Tray in the bottom position. 3. Add the eggplant to it and close the lid. Move SmartSwitch to AIR FRY/STOVETOP, set the cooking temperature to 400 degrees F and the cooking time to 10 minutes. 4. Remove the eggplant and be sure to clean out any pieces of eggplant. 5. Spray a baking pan with nonstick cooking spray. Place half the eggplant in the pan and top with half the marinara sauce, ricotta, and mozzarella. 6. Repeat with the remaining eggplant, sauce, and cheeses. 7. BAKE the food at 400 degrees F for 12 minutes; after 10 minutes of cooking time, top the casserole with the breadcrumbs. 8. Allow the casserole to cool for 5 to 10 minutes when done. 9. Serve warm.

Per Serving: Calories 496; Fat: 28.82g; Sodium: 1873mg; Carbs: 41.59g; Fiber: 12.3g; Sugar: 22.68g; Protein: 20.61g

Black Olives & Beans Tortillas

Prep Time: 10 minutes | Cook Time: 10 minutes | Serves: 4

- 6 oz. (170g) pitted black olives, sliced
- Juice of ½ lime
- 1 tsp. ground cumin
- 15oz. (420g) vegetarian refried beans (Trader Joe's recommended)
- 12 small flour tortillas, warmed
- Guacamole (optional)

1. In a small bowl, combine the olives, lime juice, and cumin. 2. Place 2 tablespoons of refried beans in the center of each tortilla. Sprinkle some of the olive mixture over the top. 3. Roll up each tortilla, tucking the edges under the bottom to seal. Spray the tortillas with nonstick canola oil. 4. Place the Crisper Tray in the bottom position. Add the taquitos to it and close the lid. Move SmartSwitch to AIR FRY/STOVETOP, set the cooking temperature to 340 degrees F and the cooking time to 5 minutes. 5. You can cook the taquitos in batches. 6. Transfer the taquitos to a platter. Serve immediately with the guacamole (if using).

Per Serving: Calories 562; Fat: 15.39g; Sodium: 2128mg; Carbs: 88.85g; Fiber: 10g; Sugar: 5.69g; Protein: 17.41g

Cheese Bowtie Pasta Bake

Prep Time: 20 minutes | Cook Time: 10 minutes | Serves: 4

8 oz. (225g) bowtie pasta (makes 4 cups cooked)
2 cups roasted vegetables
1 cup marinara sauce
⅓ cup shredded vegan mozzarella-style cheese
½ tsp. dried oregano

1. Cook the pasta according to the package directions. Drain well. 2. In a large bowl, combine the pasta, roasted vegetables, and marinara sauce. 3. Place the pasta mixture in a suitable spring-form pan. Sprinkle the mozzarella and oregano over the top. 4. Place the Crisper Tray in the bottom position. Place the pan on the tray and close the lid. 5. Move SmartSwitch to AIR FRY/STOVETOP, and then use the center front arrows to select BAKE/ROAST. Set the cooking temperature to 370 degrees F and the cooking time to 8 minutes. 6. When cooked, the mozzarella should be melted and the edges should be crispy. 7. Allow the pasta bake to cool slightly before serving

Per Serving: Calories 128; Fat: 0.92g; Sodium: 741mg; Carbs: 25.5g; Fiber: 4.7g; Sugar: 6.36g; Protein: 6.64g

Cheese Black Bean Quesadillas

Prep Time: 10 minutes | Cook Time: 10 minutes | Serves: 4

8 small flour tortillas (regular or whole grain)
1½ cups shredded vegan Cheddar-style or mozzarella-style cheese
1 cup canned black beans, drained and rinsed
½ cup chopped fresh cilantro
Salsa

1. In the center of each tortilla, place an equal amount of cheese, beans, and cilantro. Fold the tortillas in half. 2. Place the Crisper Tray in the bottom position. Add the tortillas to it and close the lid. 3. Move SmartSwitch to AIR FRY/STOVETOP, set the cooking temperature to 380 degrees F and the cooking time to 5 minutes. 4. The cheese should be melted and the tops should be golden and crispy when cooked. 5. Transfer the quesadillas to a platter and serve immediately with the salsa.

Per Serving: Calories 393; Fat: 5.76g; Sodium: 992mg; Carbs: 59.95g; Fiber: 6.9g; Sugar: 3.84g; Protein: 24.76g

Cauliflower Casserole

Prep Time: 20 minutes | Cook Time: 17 minutes | Serves: 4

1 head of cauliflower, trimmed and chopped
¼ tsp. kosher salt
1 tbsp. olive oil
4 cups cooked elbow macaroni
½ cup shredded vegan mozzarella-style cheese (Daiya recommended)
Red pepper flakes (optional)

For The Sauce

1 cup raw cashews
Juice of 2 lemons
14oz. (400g) canned coconut milk
2 tbsp. nutritional yeast
¼ tsp. garlic powder
1 tsp. kosher salt
½ tsp. freshly ground black pepper

1. To make the cream sauce, place the cashews in a medium bowl, cover with boiling water, and soak for 15 minutes. 2. Drain the water and transfer the cashews to a blender. 3. Add the lemon juice, coconut milk, nutritional yeast, garlic powder, salt, and pepper. Blend them until smooth. Set aside. 4. Spray 4 mini loaf pans with nonstick cooking spray. Set aside. 5. In a large bowl, combine the cauliflower, olive oil, and salt. 6. Place the Crisper Tray in the bottom position. Add the cauliflower to it and close the lid. 7. Move SmartSwitch to AIR FRY/STOVETOP, set the cooking temperature to 400 degrees F and the cooking time to 5 minutes. 8. Transfer the cooked cauliflower to a large bowl. Add the pasta and 1 cup of the sauce. Evenly divide the pasta mixture among the 4 pans. 9. Sprinkle an equal amount of cheese over each mixture. (Refrigerate the remaining sauce for up to 5 days.) 10. BAKE them in batches at 400 degrees F for 5 to 6 minutes until the cheese melts. 11. Allow the casseroles to cool slightly. Serve with the red pepper flakes (if using).

Per Serving: Calories 673; Fat: 33.76g; Sodium: 1242mg; Carbs: 72.57g; Fiber: 7.7g; Sugar: 9.7g; Protein: 25.7g

Spanish Rice Taquitos

Prep Time: 15 minutes | Cook Time: 10 minutes | Serves: 3

1 cup cooked brown rice, warmed
1 packet Sazón Goya seasoning
½ cup frozen green peas
12 medium corn tortillas
1 red bell pepper, sliced into 12 strips
Guacamole

1. In a small bowl, combine the brown rice, seasoning, and peas. 2. Spread 2 tablespoons of the rice mixture in the center of each tortilla. Add a bell pepper strip to each tortilla. 3. Roll up the tortillas, tucking the edges under to seal. 4. Place the Crisper Tray in the bottom position. 5. Add the food to it and close the lid. Move SmartSwitch to AIR FRY/STOVETOP, set the cooking temperature to 340 degrees F and the cooking time to 4 minutes. 6. Serve the dish warm with the guacamole.

Per Serving: Calories 308; Fat: 3.48g; Sodium: 142mg; Carbs: 62.7g; Fiber: 8.6g; Sugar: 3.09g; Protein: 8.64g

Chapter 3 Snacks and Appetizers Recipes

Spicy Olives 40	Crusted Avocado Wedges 45
Zucchini Chips 40	Blooming Onion with Sauce 46
Lemon Mushrooms 41	Beet Chips 46
Spicy Pecans 41	Sweet Potato Chips with Parsley 47
Jalapeño Poppers Wrapped in Bacon 42	Tomato Bruschetta 47
Brussels Sprouts with Bacon 42	Mini Cheese Sandwiches 48
Crispy Brussels Sprout Pieces 43	Russet Potato Skins........................48
Seasoned Kale Chips 43	Buffalo Cauliflower Wings 49
Delicious Corn Fritters 44	Buffalo Cauliflower Bites 49
Avocado & Black Bean Rolls 44	Fried Pickles with Dressing 50
Corn Salsa 45	Spiced Kale Chips 50

Spicy Olives

Prep Time: 10 minutes | Cook Time: 5 minutes | Serves: 4

12 ounces (340 g) pitted black extra-large olives
¼ cup (31 g) all-purpose flour
1 cup (50 g) panko bread crumbs
2 teaspoons dried thyme
1 teaspoon red pepper flakes
1 teaspoon smoked paprika
1 egg beaten with 1 tablespoon (15 ml) water
Vegetable oil for spraying

1. Drain the olives and place them on a paper towel–lined plate to dry. 2. Place the flour on a plate. Combine the panko, thyme, red pepper flakes, and paprika on a separate plate. 3. Dip an olive in the flour, shaking off any excess, then coat with egg mixture. 4. Dredge the olive in the panko mixture, pressing to make the crumbs adhere, and place the breaded olive on a plate. 5. Repeat with the remaining olives. 6. Place the Crisper Tray in the bottom position. Add the olives to it, spray them with oil and and close the lid. 7. Move SmartSwitch to AIR FRY/STOVETOP, set the cooking temperature to 400 degrees F and the cooking time to 5 minutes. 8. The breading should be browned and crispy. 9. Serve warm.

Per Serving: Calories 168; Fat: 10.58g; Sodium: 684mg; Carbs: 16.15g; Fiber: 3.4g; Sugar: 0.65g; Protein: 3.79g

Zucchini Chips

Prep Time: 15 minutes | Cook Time: 10 minutes | Serves: 6

2 large eggs
1 cup finely ground blanched almond flour
½ cup Parmesan cheese
1½ teaspoons sea salt
1 teaspoon garlic powder
½ teaspoon smoked paprika
¼ teaspoon freshly ground black pepper
2 zucchini, cut into ¼-inch-thick slices
Avocado oil spray

1. Beat the eggs in a shallow bowl. 2. In another bowl, stir together the almond flour, Parmesan cheese, salt, garlic powder, smoked paprika, and black pepper. 3. Dip the zucchini slices in the egg mixture, then coat them with the almond flour mixture. 4. Place the Crisper Tray in the bottom position. 5. Add the zucchini chips to it and close the lid. Move SmartSwitch to AIR FRY/STOVETOP, set the cooking temperature to 400 degrees F and the cooking time to 10 minutes. 6. Flip the zucchini chips and spray them with oil after 4 minutes of cooking time. 7. Serve the chips with your favorite dipping sauce.

Per Serving: Calories 205; Fat: 16.64g; Sodium: 761mg; Carbs: 6.44g; Fiber: 2.6g; Sugar: 1.3g; Protein: 9.8g

Lemon Mushrooms

Prep Time: 10 minutes | Cook Time: 15 minutes | Serves: 6

12 ounces sliced mushrooms
1 tablespoon avocado oil
Sea salt
Freshly ground black pepper
3 tablespoons unsalted butter
1 teaspoon minced garlic
1 teaspoon freshly squeezed lemon juice
½ teaspoon red pepper flakes
2 tablespoons chopped fresh parsley

1. Place the mushrooms in a medium bowl and toss with the oil. Season them to taste with salt and pepper. 2. Place the Crisper Tray in the bottom position. 3. Add the mushrooms to it in a single layer and close the lid. 4. Move SmartSwitch to AIR FRY/STOVETOP, set the cooking temperature to 375 degrees F and the cooking time to 15 minutes. 5. Melt the butter in a small pot over medium-low heat. Stir in the garlic and cook for 30 seconds. 6. Remove the pot from the heat and stir in the lemon juice and red pepper flakes. 7. Toss the mushrooms with the lemon-garlic butter and garnish with the parsley before serving.

Per Serving: Calories 71; Fat: 6.41g; Sodium: 32mg; Carbs: 2.51g; Fiber: 0.7g; Sugar: 1.35g; Protein: 2.13g

Spicy Pecans

Prep Time: 7 minutes | Cook Time: 15 minutes | Serves: 8

3 tablespoons unsalted butter, melted
¼ cup brown sugar substitute, such as Swerve or Sukrin Gold
1½ teaspoons Maldon sea salt (or regular sea salt if you like)
¼ teaspoon cayenne pepper, more or less to taste
2 cups pecan halves

1. Place the melted butter in a small pot and whisk in the brown sugar substitute, sea salt, and cayenne pepper. Stir them until well combined. 2. Place the pecans in a medium bowl and pour the butter mixture over them. Toss them to coat. 3. Place the Crisper Tray in the bottom position. Add the pecans to it in a single layer and close the lid. 4. Move SmartSwitch to AIR FRY/STOVETOP, set the cooking temperature to 275 degrees F and the cooking time to 15 minutes. 5. Stir the pecans after 10 minutes of cooking time. 6. Transfer the pecans to a parchment paper–lined baking sheet and allow them to cool completely before serving. 7. You can store them in an airtight container at room temperature for up to 7 days.

Per Serving: Calories 200; Fat: 20.72g; Sodium: 442mg; Carbs: 4.02g; Fiber: 2.4g; Sugar: 1.02g; Protein: 2.47g

Jalapeño Poppers Wrapped in Bacon

Prep Time: 15 minutes | Cook Time: 25 minutes | Serves: 12

12 jalapeño peppers
8 ounces cream cheese, at room temperature
2 tablespoons minced onion
1 teaspoon garlic powder
½ teaspoon smoked paprika
Sea salt
Freshly ground black pepper
12 strips bacon

1. Slice the jalapeños in half lengthwise, then seed them and remove any remaining white membranes to make room for the filling. 2. Place the Crisper Tray in the bottom position. Add the jalapeños to it in a single layer and close the lid. 3. Move SmartSwitch to AIR FRY/STOVETOP, set the cooking temperature to 400 degrees F and the cooking time to 7 minutes. 4. Remove the peppers and place them on a paper towel, cut-side up. Allow them to rest until they are cool enough to handle. 5. Stir together the cream cheese, minced onion, garlic powder, and smoked paprika in a medium bowl. Season them with salt and pepper. 6. Spoon the cream cheese filling into the jalapeños. 7. Cut the bacon strips in half, and wrap 1 piece around each stuffed jalapeño half. 8. Place the bacon-wrapped jalapeños with the cut-side up on the tray in a single layer, and then AIR-FRY them for 10 to 15 minutes more until the bacon is crispy. 9. Serve warm.

Per Serving: Calories 91; Fat: 6.99g; Sodium: 172mg; Carbs: 5.63g; Fiber: 0.9g; Sugar: 3.04g; Protein: 2.85g

Brussels Sprouts with Bacon

Prep Time: 15 minutes | Cook Time: 10 minutes | Serves: 6

1 pound Brussels sprouts, trimmed and halved
1 tablespoon avocado oil
1 tablespoon coconut aminos
1 teaspoon garlic powder
1 teaspoon smoked paprika
Sea salt
Freshly ground black pepper
4 strips cooked bacon, crumbled

1. Place the Brussels sprouts in a large bowl and toss them with the avocado oil, coconut aminos, garlic powder, smoked paprika, salt, and pepper. 2. Place the Crisper Tray in the bottom position. Add the Brussels sprouts in a single layer to it and close the lid. 3. Move SmartSwitch to AIR FRY/STOVETOP, set the cooking temperature to 375 degrees F and the cooking time to 18 minutes. 4. Stir them halfway through cooking. 5. Transfer the sprouts to a bowl and toss with the bacon. Enjoy.

Per Serving: Calories 67; Fat: 3.6g; Sodium: 97mg; Carbs: 7.65g; Fiber: 3.2g; Sugar: 1.78g; Protein: 3.27g

Crispy Brussels Sprout Pieces

Prep Time: 5 minutes | **Cook Time:** 16 minutes | **Serves:** 4

1 lb (450g) Brussels sprouts, trimmed and halved or quartered
1 tbsp. olive oil
¾ tsp. kosher salt
¾ tsp. freshly ground black pepper

1. In a large bowl, combine the Brussels sprouts, olive oil, salt, and pepper. Toss them well to coat. 2. Place the Crisper Tray in the bottom position. Add the Brussels sprouts to it and close the lid. 3. Move SmartSwitch to AIR FRY/STOVETOP, set the cooking temperature to 390 degrees F and the cooking time to 16 minutes. 4. Transfer the caramelized and tender Brussels sprouts to a serving bowl and allow the dish to cool slightly. Enjoy.

Per Serving: Calories 80; Fat: 3.73g; Sodium: 465mg; Carbs: 10.42g; Fiber: 4.4g; Sugar: 2.5g; Protein: 3.88g

Seasoned Kale Chips

Prep Time: 15 minutes | **Cook Time:** 15 minutes | **Serves:** 8

1 bunch kale, washed, stemmed, and torn into pieces
1 tablespoon extra-virgin olive oil
2 teaspoons everything seasoning

1. Place the kale leaves in a large bowl, and toss them with the olive oil and seasoning. 2. Place the Crisper Tray in the bottom position. 3. Add the kale leaves to it in a single layer and close the lid. 4. Move SmartSwitch to AIR FRY/STOVETOP, set the cooking temperature to 325 degrees F and the cooking time to 7 minutes. 5. Stir the food halfway through cooking. 6. You can cook them in batches. 7. Serve and enjoy.

Per Serving: Calories 10; Fat: 0.77g; Sodium: 67mg; Carbs: 0.59g; Fiber: 0.2g; Sugar: 0.12g; Protein: 0.12g

Delicious Corn Fritters

Prep Time: 10 Minutes | Cook Time: 10 Minutes | Serves: 3

- 2 tbsp. all-purpose flour
- 2 tbsp. cornmeal
- ¼ tsp. baking powder
- ½ tsp. kosher salt
- 2 tbsp. tahini
- 3 tbsp. low-sodium vegetable broth
- 1 tsp. chopped fresh thyme
- 1 tsp. rice vinegar
- 1 cup corn kernels
- ½ cup finely chopped broccoli

1. Whisk together the flour, cornmeal, baking powder, and salt in a medium bowl. Add the tahini, vegetable broth, thyme, rice vinegar, corn, and broccoli. 2. With clean hands, divide the mixture into 6 equally sized patties. 3. Place the Crisper Tray in the bottom position. Add the fritters to it and close the lid. 4. Move SmartSwitch to AIR FRY/STOVETOP, set the cooking temperature to 390 degrees F and the cooking time to 10 minutes. 5. Flip the fritters halfway through. 6. Let the dish cool for 3 to 5 minutes before serving.

Per Serving: Calories 147; Fat: 6.38g; Sodium: 512mg; Carbs: 20.59g; Fiber: 2.9g; Sugar: 1.97g; Protein: 4.34g

Avocado & Black Bean Rolls

Prep Time: 10 minutes | Cook Time: 6 minutes | Serves: 4

- 1 large avocado, diced
- ½ cup black beans, rinsed and drained
- 2 tbsp. salsa, plus more
- ¼ cup corn kernels
- 2 tbsp. chopped fresh cilantro
- 8 egg roll wrappers

1. In a medium bowl, combine the avocado, black beans, salsa, corn, and cilantro. 2. Place 2 tablespoons of the mixture in the center of each egg roll wrapper. 3. Fold a corner over the filling, tuck in the sides, and roll up from the bottom to the top. 4. Wet the top with water to help secure the seal. 5. Spray the egg rolls with canola oil. 6. Place the Crisper Tray in the bottom position. Add the rolls to it and close the lid. 7. Move SmartSwitch to AIR FRY/STOVETOP, set the cooking temperature to 300 degrees F and the cooking time to 6 minutes. 8. Flip the food halfway through. 9. Serve the dish with more salsa.

Per Serving: Calories 359; Fat: 8.83g; Sodium: 453mg; Carbs: 58.63g; Fiber: 8.7g; Sugar: 1.45g; Protein: 12.9g

Corn Salsa

Prep Time: 10 minutes | Cook Time: 10 minutes | Serves: 6

- 2 cups frozen corn kernels
- ½ cup finely chopped bell pepper (any color)
- ½ cup finely chopped red onion
- 1 garlic clove, finely chopped
- 1 tbsp. olive oil
- 1 tsp. kosher salt
- 3 tbsp. chopped pickled jalapeños
- ½ cup roughly chopped fresh cilantro
- Tortilla chips

1. In a medium bowl, combine the corn, bell pepper, onion, garlic, olive oil, and salt. 2. Place the Crisper Tray in the bottom position. Add the food to it and close the lid. 3. Move SmartSwitch to AIR FRY/STOVETOP, set the cooking temperature to 400 degrees F and the cooking time to 8 minutes. 4. Transfer the salsa to a large bowl and mix in the jalapeños and cilantro. 5. Serve immediately with the tortilla chips.

Per Serving: Calories 129; Fat: 6.05g; Sodium: 474mg; Carbs: 16.99g; Fiber: 1.6g; Sugar: 3.36g; Protein: 2.18g

Crusted Avocado Wedges

Prep Time: 15 minutes | Cook Time: 15 minutes | Serves: 8

- 2 medium ripe avocados, halved and pitted
- ½ cup aquafaba (from a 15oz. [420g] can of chickpeas)
- 1½ cups panko breadcrumbs
- ½ tsp. kosher salt

1. Slice each avocado into 8 wedges. 2. Place the aquafaba and breadcrumbs in separate medium bowls. 3. Dip the wedges in the aquafaba and then in the breadcrumbs. 4. Place the Crisper Tray in the bottom position. Add the aquafaba to it and close the lid. 5. Move SmartSwitch to AIR FRY/STOVETOP, set the cooking temperature to 390 degrees F and the cooking time to 6 minutes. 6. Transfer the wedges to a platter and sprinkle the salt over the top. Serve immediately.

Per Serving: Calories 129; Fat: 8.14g; Sodium: 155mg; Carbs: 12.46g; Fiber: 4.9g; Sugar: 1.7g; Protein: 3.62g

Blooming Onion with Sauce

Prep Time: 10 minutes | Cook Time: 25 minutes | Serves: 4

½ cup aquafaba (from a 15oz. [420g] can of chickpeas)
½ cup all-purpose flour
¼ tsp. kosher salt
½ cup seasoned breadcrumbs
1 large Vidalia onion

For The Sauce
2 tbsp. vegan mayonnaise
2 tbsp. dairy-free plain yogurt
2 tbsp. ketchup
1 to 2 tsp. sriracha chili sauce

1. Place the aquafaba in a medium shallow bowl. 2. In a separate medium bowl, combine the flour, salt, and breadcrumbs. 3. Slice the top off the onion and turn it over to rest on a flat surface. 4. Cut several slits around the entire onion, then turn it over and gently spread out the petals. 5. Dip the onion in the aquafaba and then in the flour mixture. 6. Sprinkle the flour mixture in between the petals and shake off any excess. Spray the onion with canola oil. 7. Place the Crisper Tray in the bottom position. Add the food to it and close the lid. 8. Move SmartSwitch to AIR FRY/STOVETOP, set the cooking temperature to 380 degrees F and the cooking time to 22 minutes. 9. In a small bowl, make the yum yum sauce by whisking together the ingredients until smooth. 10. Transfer the blooming onion to a platter and serve immediately with the sauce.

Per Serving: Calories 260; Fat: 4.35g; Sodium: 1543mg; Carbs: 44.28g; Fiber: 6.6g; Sugar: 8.54g; Protein: 8.75g

Beet Chips

Prep Time: 10 minutes | Cook Time: 25 minutes | Serves: 4

4 medium red and golden beets, trimmed and peeled
Sea salt

For The Sauce
1 cup raw cashews, soaked in water for at least 2 hours or overnight
Juice of ½ lemon
1 cup water
1 tsp. kosher salt
¼ tsp. garlic powder
¼ cup chopped fresh dill

1. In a blender, make the dill sauce by combining the cashews, lemon juice, and water. Blend until smooth. Add the kosher salt, garlic powder, and dill. 2. Blend them for a few seconds more. Place the sauce in a serving bowl and set aside. 3. Cut the beets into ⅛-inch slices. Spray the beets with canola oil. 4. Place the Crisper Tray in the bottom position. Add the beet slices to it and close the lid. 5. Move SmartSwitch to AIR FRY/STOVETOP, set the cooking temperature to 315 degrees F and the cooking time to 12 minutes. 6. Toss the food halfway through. 7. Transfer the beets to a platter and allow to cool. Sprinkle the sea salt over the chips. Serve the dish with 1 cup of the dill sauce. 8. You can refrigerate the remaining sauce for up to 3 days.

Per Serving: Calories 427; Fat: 34.1g; Sodium: 875mg; Carbs: 27.83g; Fiber: 4.3g; Sugar: 11.52g; Protein: 9.15g

Sweet Potato Chips with Parsley

Prep Time: 10 minutes | Cook Time: 25 minutes | Serves: 8

2 medium sweet potatoes

For The Tapenade

1 cup pitted green or black olives

¼ cup sun-dried tomatoes, packed in oil, drained and chopped

2 tbsp. chopped fresh parsley

1 tbsp. olive oil

½ tsp. kosher salt

½ tsp. freshly ground black pepper

Chopped fresh parsley

1. In a food processor, make the tapenade by combining the ingredients. Pulse until well combined. Transfer the tapenade to a medium bowl and set aside. 2. Cut the sweet potatoes into ⅛-inch slices. 3. Place the Crisper Tray in the bottom position. Add the potato slices to it and close the lid. 4. Move SmartSwitch to AIR FRY/STOVETOP, set the cooking temperature to 350 degrees F and the cooking time to 12 minutes. 5. Toss the food halfway through. 6. Transfer the sweet potato chips to a platter to cool. Top them with the tapenade and sprinkle the parsley over the top before serving.

Per Serving: Calories 52; Fat: 1.91g; Sodium: 170mg; Carbs: 8.27g; Fiber: 1.5g; Sugar: 2.88g; Protein: 1.03g

Tomato Bruschetta

Prep Time: 10 minutes | Cook Time: 11 minutes | Serves: 8

6 large garlic cloves, peeled

1 tbsp. olive oil

1 tsp. kosher salt, divided, plus more

1 pint (300g) cherry tomatoes, quartered

¼ cup chopped fresh basil

2 tbsp. balsamic vinegar, plus more

1 baguette

1. Toss the garlic with olive oil and ½ teaspoon of salt. 2. Place the Crisper Tray in the bottom position. Add the garlic to it and close the lid. 3. Move SmartSwitch to AIR FRY/STOVETOP, set the cooking temperature to 400 degrees F and the cooking time to 5 minutes. 4. Remove the garlic and roughly chop. 5. In a large bowl, combine the garlic, tomatoes, basil, balsamic vinegar, and the remaining ½ teaspoon of salt. 6. Cut the baguette into 16 equally sized slices. 7. AIR-FRY the slices for 2 to 3 minutes more. 8. Transfer the slices to a platter. Top with the garlic and tomato mixture. Season the dish with more salt and balsamic vinegar if desired.

Per Serving: Calories 55; Fat: 2g; Sodium: 364mg; Carbs: 7.83g; Fiber: 0.3g; Sugar: 1.31g; Protein: 1.49g

Mini Cheese Sandwiches

Prep Time: 15 minutes | Cook Time: 15 minutes | Serves: 4

- 2 tbsp. olive oil
- 1 garlic clove, minced
- 1 package of 12 dinner rolls
- 8 slices vegan Cheddar-style cheese
- 2 cups baby spinach
- 1 Granny Smith apple, cored and thinly sliced

1. In a small bowl, combine the olive oil and garlic. Set aside. 2. The rolls come connected as one large piece. Cut this piece in half and slice the 2 halves horizontally. 3. Place the Crisper Tray in the bottom position. Add 1 bottom half of rolls in the fryer basket and top with half the cheese, spinach, and apple slices to it; place 1 top half of rolls on top and brush with half of the olive oil mixture. 4. Move SmartSwitch to AIR FRY/STOVETOP, set the cooking temperature to 370 degrees F and the cooking time to 7 minutes. 5. The top should be golden brown and the cheese should be melted when cooked. 6. Transfer the rolls to a platter to cool slightly. Cut the 2 roll halves into 12 sandwiches before serving.

Per Serving: Calories 337; Fat: 26.27g; Sodium: 410mg; Carbs: 10.89g; Fiber: 1.8g; Sugar: 4.34g; Protein: 14.84g

Russet Potato Skins

Prep Time: 15 minutes | Cook Time: 40 minutes | Serves: 8

- 4 medium russet potatoes, scrubbed
- 2 tbsp. olive oil
- 1 tsp. kosher salt
- ½ tsp. freshly ground black pepper
- 1½ cups chopped broccoli
- ½ cup shredded vegan Cheddar-style cheese
- Dairy-free yogurt or sour cream (optional)

1. Poke the potatoes with a fork. 2. Place the Crisper Tray in the bottom position. Add the potatoes to it and close the lid. 3. Move SmartSwitch to AIR FRY/STOVETOP, set the cooking temperature to 390 degrees F and the cooking time to 25 minutes. 4. Remove the potatoes. Cut them in half lengthwise and scoop out some of the flesh. Brush the insides with olive oil and season with salt and pepper. 5. Top each potato skin with broccoli and cheese. 6. AIR-FRY them for 5 to 6 minutes more until the broccoli is crisp-tender and the cheese has melted. 7. Serve the dish with the yogurt (if using).

Per Serving: Calories 200; Fat: 5.38g; Sodium: 360mg; Carbs: 33.88g; Fiber: 2.6g; Sugar: 1.35g; Protein: 5.58g

Buffalo Cauliflower Wings

Prep Time: 20 minutes | Cook Time: 15 minutes | Serves: 6

1 head cauliflower
3 large eggs
¾ cup finely ground blanched almond flour
¾ cup finely grated Parmesan cheese
1 teaspoon garlic powder
½ teaspoon smoked paprika
½ teaspoon sea salt
½ teaspoon freshly ground black pepper
Avocado oil spray
1 cup Buffalo hot sauce, such as Frank's RedHot
4 tablespoons unsalted butter
Garlic Ranch Dressing or Blue Cheese Dressing, for serving

1. Line a baking sheet or platter with parchment paper. 2. Core the cauliflower and cut it into large florets. 3. Beat the eggs together in a small bowl. 4. In a separate bowl, combine the almond flour, Parmesan, garlic powder, smoked paprika, salt, and pepper. 5. Dip a cauliflower floret into the egg, and then coat it in the almond flour mixture, making sure to firmly press the mixture into the cauliflower. 6. Transfer the coated floret to the prepared baking sheet. Continue with the remaining cauliflower, egg, and almond flour mixture. 7. Place the Crisper Tray in the bottom position. 8. Add the cauliflower florets to it and spray them with oil. 8. Move SmartSwitch to AIR FRY/STOVETOP, set the cooking temperature to 400 degrees F and the cooking time to 12 minutes. 9. Flip the food and spray them with oil after 5 minutes of cooking time. 10. Place the hot sauce and butter in a small saucepan over medium-low heat. Heat, stirring occasionally, until the butter melts. 11. Toss the crispy cauliflower in the sauce, then use a slotted spoon to transfer the coated cauliflower to a plate or platter. 12. Serve the dish warm with the dressing.

Per Serving: Calories 244; Fat: 17.85g; Sodium: 1380mg; Carbs: 11.04g; Fiber: 3g; Sugar: 2.44g; Protein: 12.51g

Buffalo Cauliflower Bites

Prep Time: 10 minutes | Cook Time: 20 minutes | Serves: 8

2 tbsp. vegan butter (Earth Balance recommended), melted
2 tbsp. hot sauce (Frank's RedHot recommended)
1 large head of cauliflower, trimmed and chopped
1 cup panko breadcrumbs

1. In a large bowl, combine the butter and hot sauce. Add the cauliflower and toss well to coat. 2. Place the Crisper Tray in the bottom position. Add the cauliflower to it and close the lid. 3. Move SmartSwitch to AIR FRY/STOVETOP, set the cooking temperature to 360 degrees F and the cooking time to 12 minutes. 4. In a clean large bowl, combine the cauliflower and breadcrumbs. Toss them gently to coat. 5. AIR-FRY them for 5 to 7 minutes more until the breadcrumbs are golden brown. 6. Transfer the cauliflower to a platter and serve immediately.

Per Serving: Calories 88; Fat: 3.7g; Sodium: 163mg; Carbs: 11.67g; Fiber: 1.4g; Sugar: 1.65g; Protein: 2.54g

Fried Pickles with Dressing

Prep Time: 10 minutes | Cook Time: 10 minutes | Serves: 6-8

Buttermilk-Herb Ranch Dressing
¾ cup (175 g) mayonnaise
½ cup (115 g) sour cream
¼ cup (60 ml) buttermilk
¼ cup (25 g) chopped scallions
2 tablespoons (8 g) chopped fresh dill
1 tablespoon (3 g) chopped chives
½ teaspoon garlic powder
½ teaspoon onion powder
½ teaspoon cayenne pepper
Kosher salt and pepper to taste
Fried Pickles
1 jar (32 ounces, or 905 g) kosher dill pickles
¾ cup (94 g) all-purpose flour
Kosher salt and pepper to taste
2½ cups (125 g) panko bread crumbs
2 eggs beaten with 2 tablespoons (30 ml) water
Vegetable oil for spraying

1. In a medium bowl, whisk together the mayonnaise, sour cream, and buttermilk. Add the scallions, herbs, and seasonings and stir to combine. Cover the bowl and chill for at least 30 minutes prior to serving to allow the flavors to develop. 2. Cut each pickle into 4 spears and place the spears on paper towels to drain for at least 15 minutes. 3. Place the flour on a plate and season with salt and pepper. 4. Place the panko on a separate plate. 5. Dip a pickle spear in the flour, shaking off any excess, then coat with egg mixture. 6. Dredge the spear in the panko, pressing to make the crumbs adhere, and place the breaded spear on a lined baking sheet. Repeat with the remaining spears. 7. Spray the spears with oil. 8. Place the Crisper Tray in the bottom position. Add the spears to it and close the lid. Move SmartSwitch to AIR FRY/STOVETOP, set the cooking temperature to 400 degrees F and the cooking time to 10 minutes. 9. Flip them halfway through. 10. Serve the dish with buttermilk ranch dressing.

Per Serving: Calories 273; Fat: 13.16g; Sodium: 5053mg; Carbs: 33.36g; Fiber: 7.4g; Sugar: 8.35g; Protein: 9.25g

Spiced Kale Chips

Prep Time: 10 minutes | Cook Time: 10 minutes | Serves: 4

5 cups packed kale leaves, stems removed
2 tsp. canola oil
½ tsp. chili powder
½ tsp. kosher salt

1. In a large bowl, combine the kale and canola oil. Add the chili powder and salt. Gently massage the leaves with the spices. 2. Place the Crisper Tray in the bottom position. Add the food to it and close the lid. 3. Move SmartSwitch to AIR FRY/STOVETOP, set the cooking temperature to 370 degrees F and the cooking time to 5 minutes. 4. Toss the food halfway through. 5. Transfer the chips to a platter and allow them to cool before serving.

Per Serving: Calories 31; Fat: 2.49g; Sodium: 308mg; Carbs: 1.92g; Fiber: 0.8g; Sugar: 0.48g; Protein: 0.9g

Chapter 4 Poultry Recipes

Turkey Burgers with Potato Fries 52

Spanish Chicken & Peppers 52

Stuffed Turkey Meatballs 53

Prosciutto-Wrapped Chicken with Squash 53

Butter Turkey Breast 54

Turkey Breast Tenderloin 54

Chicken Meatloaf 55

Boneless Chicken Thighs 55

Stuffed Chicken Breasts 56

Pineapple Chicken 56

Classic Chicken Kebab 57

Turkey Meatballs 57

Spiced Chicken Shawarma 58

Spinach Chicken Pizza 58

Lemon Chicken Thighs 59

Simple Turkey Meatballs 59

Crusted Turkey Cutlets 60

Turkey Burgers with Potato Fries

Prep Time: 15 minutes | Cook Time: 30 minutes | Serves: 4

- 1 pound ground turkey breast
- 2 cloves garlic, pressed
- ½ cup chopped cilantro
- 1 teaspoon chili powder
- ¼ teaspoon salt
- Oil in mister
- ½ avocado
- 2 teaspoons lime juice
- 4 toasted whole-grain sandwich thins
- Tomato, cucumber, lettuce, and sprouts, for serving (optional)
- Sweet Potato Fries, for serving

1. Mix turkey with garlic, cilantro, chili powder, and salt. Form into 4 (3½-inch) patties. Make a slight indentation in the center of each one. 2. Spray patties on both sides with oil. 3. Place the Crisper Tray in the bottom position. Add the patties to it and close the lid. 4. Move SmartSwitch to AIR FRY/STOVETOP, set the cooking temperature to 370 degrees F and the cooking time to 12 minutes. 5. Mash avocado with lime juice. 6. Place burgers on whole-grain sandwich thins; top with avocado and tomato, cucumber, lettuce, and sprouts, as desired. 7. Serve with Sweet Potato Fries.

Per Serving: Calories 298; Fat: 12.94g; Sodium: 335mg; Carbs: 15.61g; Fiber: 4.3g; Sugar: 2.64g; Protein: 29.34g

Spanish Chicken & Peppers

Prep Time: 10 minutes | Cook Time: 35 minutes | Serves: 2

- 1¼ pounds assorted small chicken parts, (breasts cut into halves)
- ½ pound mini sweet peppers
- 2 teaspoons olive oil
- ¼ teaspoon salt
- ¼ teaspoon pepper
- ¼ cup light mayonnaise
- ½ clove garlic, crushed with press
- ¼ teaspoon smoked paprika
- Baguette, for serving

1. In a large bowl, toss chicken and peppers with oil, salt, and pepper. 2. Place the Crisper Tray in the bottom position. Add the peppers to it and top with chicken. 3. Move SmartSwitch to AIR FRY/STOVETOP, set the cooking temperature to 375 degrees F and the cooking time to 22 minutes. 4. Turn the chicken over halfway through. When cooked, the chicken's internal temperature should reach 165 degrees F. 5. Remove the chicken and resume cooking the peppers for 2 minutes more. 6. Stir together mayonnaise, garlic, and paprika. Serve chicken and peppers with garlic mayo on a baguette.

Per Serving: Calories 642; Fat: 26.22g; Sodium: 1952mg; Carbs: 12.59g; Fiber: 2.2g; Sugar: 6.37g; Protein: 87.38g

Stuffed Turkey Meatballs

Prep Time: 25 minutes | Cook Time: 45 minutes | Serves: 6

20 ounces ground turkey
⅓ cup Italian seasoned bread crumbs
3 tablespoons milk
1 large egg
3 cloves garlic, finely chopped
1 tablespoon loosely packed fresh rosemary leaves, finely chopped
¼ teaspoon salt
⅛ teaspoon pepper
4 ounces part-skim mozzarella, cut into ½-inch cubes
Oil in mister
2 cups marinara sauce
Parsley leaves and grated Parmesan cheese, for garnish
Bread or cooked pasta, for serving

1. In a large bowl, combine turkey, bread crumbs, milk, egg, garlic, rosemary, salt, and pepper. With a 2-tablespoon scoop, scoop turkey mixture and press 1 cube mozzarella into center, sealing meat tightly around cheese. Repeat with the remaining turkey mixture and cheese. 2. Place the Crisper Tray in the bottom position. Add the meatballs to it and close the lid. 3. Move SmartSwitch to AIR FRY/STOVETOP, set the cooking temperature to 375 degrees F and the cooking time to 8 minutes. 4. Heat the marinara sauce in a medium-size saucepan. Add meatballs and simmer 12 minutes, or until meatballs are cooked through (165°F). 5. Garnish the dish with parsley and Parmesan. 6. Serve the dish with bread or over pasta.

Per Serving: Calories 559; Fat: 46.36g; Sodium: 897mg; Carbs: 10.06g; Fiber: 1.8g; Sugar: 4.39g; Protein: 25.18g

Prosciutto-Wrapped Chicken with Squash

Prep Time: 10 minutes | Cook Time: 50 minutes | Serves: 2

1 small acorn squash, peeled, seeded, and sliced
2 teaspoons olive oil
1 teaspoon fresh thyme leaves, chopped
¼ teaspoon salt
2 boneless, skinless chicken breasts (about 1 pound)
¼ teaspoon pepper
1 tablespoon grated Parmesan cheese
4 slices prosciutto
Sautéed green beans, for serving

1. Toss together acorn squash with olive oil, thyme, and salt. 2. Place the Crisper Tray in the bottom position. Add the food to it and close the lid. 3. Move SmartSwitch to AIR FRY/STOVETOP, set the cooking temperature to 375 degrees F and the cooking time to 15 minutes. 4. Toss the food halfway through. 5. Season chicken breasts with pepper; sprinkle with Parmesan. Wrap each with 2 slices prosciutto. 6. BAKE the chicken breast at 375 degrees F for 20 minutes until the internal temperature reaches 165 degrees F. 7. Place squash on top of chicken and air-fry for 3 minutes, or until heated. 8. Serve chicken and squash with sautéed green beans.

Per Serving: Calories 519; Fat: 15.68g; Sodium: 664mg; Carbs: 24.81g; Fiber: 3.4g; Sugar: 0.94g; Protein: 68.78g

Butter Turkey Breast

Prep Time: 15 minutes | Cook Time: 50 minutes | Serves: 6:

½ cup (1 stick) butter, melted
6 garlic cloves, minced
1½ teaspoons dried oregano
2 teaspoons salt
1 teaspoon freshly ground black pepper
4 pounds bone-in turkey breast

1. In a small bowl, mix together the butter, garlic, oregano, salt, and pepper. 2. Place the turkey on a plate and pour the mixture over the turkey, making sure to spread it all over until it is well coated. 3. Place the Crisper Tray in the bottom position. Add the breast to it with the breast-side down and close the lid. 4. Move SmartSwitch to AIR FRY/STOVETOP, set the cooking temperature to 350 degrees F and the cooking time to 50 minutes. 5. Turn the breast over halfway through. 6. Cool the dish for 10 minutes before cutting the meat into slices.

Per Serving: Calories 616; Fat: 36.61g; Sodium: 1076mg; Carbs: 1.42g; Fiber: 0.3g; Sugar: 0.05g; Protein: 66.61g

Turkey Breast Tenderloin

Prep Time: 15 minutes | Cook Time: 30 minutes | Serves: 4

1 pound boneless, skinless turkey breast tenderloin
1 teaspoon salt
1 teaspoon freshly ground black pepper
½ teaspoon garlic powder
Juice of 1 lemon

1. Pat the turkey dry and season it on all sides with the salt, pepper, and garlic powder. 2. Place the Crisper Tray in the bottom position. Add the meat to it and squeeze the lemon juice over the top and close the lid. 3. Move SmartSwitch to AIR FRY/STOVETOP, set the cooking temperature to 350 degrees F and the cooking time to 25 minutes. 4. Turn the meat over after 10 minutes of cooking time. 5. Let the dish sit for 10 minutes. Cut into slices and serve.

Per Serving: Calories 203; Fat: 6.5g; Sodium: 885mg; Carbs: 25.18g; Fiber: 1.9g; Sugar: 6.39g; Protein: 10.68g

Chicken Meatloaf

Prep Time: 15 Minutes | Cook Time: 30 Minutes | Serves: 4

Extra-virgin olive oil, in a spray bottle, for greasing
1 pound ground chicken
4 garlic cloves, minced
¼ cup minced onion
2 tablespoons chopped fresh basil, divided
1 tablespoon chopped fresh parsley
1 teaspoon salt
½ teaspoon freshly ground black pepper
½ teaspoon onion powder
2 tablespoons grated Parmesan cheese
½ cup whole-wheat bread crumbs
1 egg
¼ cup heavy (whipping) cream
1 cup low-sodium tomato sauce
½ teaspoon garlic powder
1 tablespoon coconut aminos
1½ teaspoons evaporated cane sugar

1. Spray a suitable baking dish with olive oil. 2. In a large bowl, mix together the chicken, garlic, minced onion, 1½ tablespoons of basil, the parsley, salt, pepper, onion powder, Parmesan cheese, bread crumbs, egg, and cream until well combined. 3. Press the mixture into the prepared baking dish. 4. In a small bowl, mix together the tomato sauce, remaining ½ tablespoon of basil, the garlic powder, coconut aminos, and sugar and spread it over the top of the meat loaf. 5. Cover the dish loosely with aluminum foil. 6. Place the Crisper Tray in the bottom position. Place the mold on the tray and close the lid. 7. Move SmartSwitch to AIR FRY/STOVETOP, and then use the center front arrows to select BAKE/ROAST. Set the cooking temperature to 400 degrees F and the cooking time to 30 minutes. 8. Remove the foil halfway through. 9. Cool the dish for 10 minutes. 10. Cut the dish into slices and serve.

Per Serving: Calories 414; Fat: 24.69g; Sodium: 858mg; Carbs: 19.27g; Fiber: 2.2g; Sugar: 6.15g; Protein: 27.4g

Boneless Chicken Thighs

Prep Time: 10 minutes | Cook Time: 15 minutes | Serves: 4

¼ cup balsamic vinegar
3 tablespoons maple syrup
1 teaspoon whole-grain mustard
3 garlic cloves, minced
½ teaspoon salt
½ teaspoon freshly ground black pepper
½ teaspoon smoked paprika
1 pound boneless, skinless chicken thighs

1. In a small bowl, whisk together the vinegar, maple syrup, mustard, garlic, salt, pepper, and paprika. 2. Place the Crisper Tray in the bottom position. Add the wings to it and brush the tops with the vinegar mixture. 3. Move SmartSwitch to AIR FRY/STOVETOP, set the cooking temperature to 375 degrees F and the cooking time to 15 minutes. 4. Flip the thighs halfway through. 5. Let the dish sit for 5 minutes before serving.

Per Serving: Calories 258; Fat: 6.54g; Sodium: 600mg; Carbs: 38.04g; Fiber: 2g; Sugar: 17.59g; Protein: 10.86g

Stuffed Chicken Breasts

Prep Time: 10 minutes | **Cook Time:** 20 minutes | **Serves:** 4

Extra-virgin olive oil, in a spray bottle, for greasing
½ cup finely chopped broccoli
2 scallions, green part only, sliced
2 garlic cloves, minced
½ cup grated cheddar cheese
¼ cup cream cheese
1 teaspoon salt
½ teaspoon freshly ground black pepper
½ teaspoon dried oregano
½ teaspoon dried basil
4 boneless, skinless chicken breasts

1. Spray a suitable baking dish with olive oil. 2. In a small bowl, mix together the broccoli, scallion, garlic, cheddar cheese, cream cheese, salt, pepper, oregano, and basil. 3. Place the chicken breasts between two pieces of plastic wrap and, using a meat mallet or a heavy can, pound the chicken to an even ½-inch thickness. 4. Scoop one-quarter of the cheese mixture onto the center of each chicken breast. Fold over each breast to cover the mixture; then place in the prepared baking dish in a single layer. 5. Place the Crisper Tray in the bottom position. Place the pan on the tray and close the lid. 6. Move SmartSwitch to AIR FRY/STOVETOP, and then use the center front arrows to select BAKE/ROAST. Set the cooking temperature to 375 degrees F and the cooking time to 20 minutes. 7. Turn the chicken over after 8 minutes of cooking time. 8. Let the dish sit for 5 minutes before serving.

Per Serving: Calories 445; Fat: 17.06g; Sodium: 879mg; Carbs: 2.26g; Fiber: 0.5g; Sugar: 0.79g; Protein: 66.69g

Pineapple Chicken

Prep Time: 10 minutes | **Cook Time:** 25 minutes | **Serves:** 4

Extra-virgin olive oil, in a spray bottle, for greasing
1 (15-ounce) can crushed pineapple, drained
2 tablespoons coconut aminos
1 tablespoon honey
3 garlic cloves, minced
½ teaspoon salt
½ teaspoon paprika
¼ teaspoon freshly ground black pepper
1 pound boneless, skinless chicken breasts

1. Spray a suitable baking dish with olive oil. 2. In a small bowl, combine the pineapple, coconut aminos, honey, garlic, salt, paprika, and pepper. 3. Place the chicken breasts in a single layer in the baking dish and spread half the pineapple mixture over the top. 4. Place the Crisper Tray in the bottom position. Place the pan on the tray and close the lid. 5. Move SmartSwitch to AIR FRY/STOVETOP, and then use the center front arrows to select BAKE/ROAST. Set the cooking temperature to 360 degrees F and the cooking time to 24 minutes. 6. Turn the chicken over and spread the remaining pineapple mixture over the chicken after 8 minutes of cooking time. 7. The chicken should reach an internal temperature of 160 degrees F when cooked. 8. Let the dish sit for 5 minutes before serving.

Per Serving: Calories 410; Fat: 6.63g; Sodium: 605mg; Carbs: 76.4g; Fiber: 2.7g; Sugar: 57g; Protein: 12.17g

Lemon Chicken Thighs

Prep Time: 5 minutes | Cook Time: 25 minutes | Serves: 4

- 4 bone-in chicken thighs, skin and fat removed
- 2 tablespoons olive oil
- 1 teaspoon garlic powder
- 1 teaspoon salt
- Black pepper
- 1 lemon, sliced

1. Coat the chicken thighs in the olive oil, garlic powder, and salt. 2. Tear off four pieces of aluminum foil, with each sheet being large enough to envelop one chicken thigh. 3. Place one chicken thigh onto each piece of foil, season them with black pepper, and then top it with slices of lemon. 4. Place the Crisper Tray in the bottom position. Place the food on the tray and close the lid. 5. Move SmartSwitch to AIR FRY/STOVETOP, and then use the center front arrows to select BAKE/ROAST. Set the cooking temperature to 380 degrees F and the cooking time to 22 minutes. 6. Carefully open each packet to avoid a steam burn. Serve and enjoy.

Per Serving: Calories 491; Fat: 38.84g; Sodium: 738mg; Carbs: 1.89g; Fiber: 0.1g; Sugar: 0.32g; Protein: 32.06g

Simple Turkey Meatballs

Prep Time: 5 minutes | Cook Time: 15 minutes | Serves: 4

- 1 pound ground turkey
- 1 egg
- ¼ teaspoon red pepper flakes
- ¼ cup whole wheat bread crumbs
- 1 teaspoon salt
- ½ teaspoon garlic powder
- ½ teaspoon onion powder
- ½ teaspoon black pepper

1. In a large bowl, combine all of the ingredients and mix well. 2. Divide the meatball mixture into 12 portions. Roll each portion into a ball. 3. Place the Crisper Tray in the bottom position. Add the balls to it and close the lid. 4. Move SmartSwitch to AIR FRY/STOVETOP, set the cooking temperature to 360 degrees F and the cooking time to 12 minutes. 5. Serve the browned meatballs warm.

Per Serving: Calories 610; Fat: 53.2g; Sodium: 707mg; Carbs: 6.15g; Fiber: 0.5g; Sugar: 0.76g; Protein: 24.92g

Crusted Turkey Cutlets

Prep Time: 5 minutes | Cook Time: 10 minutes | Serves: 4

½ cup whole wheat bread crumbs
¼ teaspoon paprika
¼ teaspoon salt
¼ teaspoon black pepper
⅛ teaspoon dried sage
⅛ teaspoon garlic powder
1 egg
4 turkey breast cutlets
Chopped fresh parsley, for serving

1. In a medium shallow bowl, whisk together the bread crumbs, paprika, salt, black pepper, sage, and garlic powder. 2. In a separate medium shallow bowl, whisk the egg until frothy. 3. Dip each turkey cutlet into the egg mixture, then into the bread crumb mixture, coating the outside with the crumbs. 4. Place the Crisper Tray in the bottom position. Place the breaded turkey cutlets in a single layer on the tray and close the lid. 5. Move SmartSwitch to AIR FRY/STOVETOP, and then use the center front arrows to select BAKE/ROAST. Set the cooking temperature to 380 degrees F and the cooking time to 8 minutes. 6. Flip the cutlets halfway through. 7. When cooked, the cutlets should reach an internal temperature of 380 degrees F. 8. Sprinkle the parsley over the dish and serve.

Per Serving: Calories 316; Fat: 13.4g; Sodium: 356mg; Carbs: 10.25g; Fiber: 0.7g; Sugar: 1.02g; Protein: 36.06g

Chapter 5 Pork, Beef and Lamb Recipes

Steak with Onion Gravy 62

Simple-Spiced Pork Chops 62

Beef Empanadas 63

Easy Pork Tenderloin 63

Spice-Rubbed Ribeye 64

Tzatziki Lamb Kofta 64

Crusted Pork Tenderloin with Potatoes ... 65

Deconstructed Chicago Hot Dogs 65

Glazed Baby Back Ribs 66

Butter Pork Tenderloin Chopps 66

Savory Pork Shoulder 67

Pecan Pork Stuffing.......................... 67

Mustard Pork Chops 68

African Pork Shoulder 68

Bacon Cheeseburger Casserole 69

Pork Milanese 69

Sausages with Peppers and Onions 70

Healthy Scotch Eggs 70

Savory Sausage Cobbler 71

Pork Chops with Scallions 71

Onion & Beef Stuffed Peppers 72

Steak Salad with Blue Cheese Dressing ... 72

Lamb Kofta with Yogurt Sauce 73

Beef Tips with Onions 73

Lebanese Malfouf 74

Cheese Beef Stuffed Peppers 74

Steak with Onion Gravy

Prep Time: 15 minutes | Cook Time: 5 minutes | Serves: 4

Onion Gravy

1 tablespoon (14 g) unsalted butter
1 tablespoon (15 ml) vegetable oil
1 yellow onion, thinly sliced
Kosher salt and pepper to taste
2 tablespoons (16 g) all-purpose flour
2 cups (480 ml) chicken broth, warmed
½ teaspoon Worcestershire sauce

Country-Fried Steak

½ cup (63 g) all-purpose flour
1 teaspoon kosher salt
½ teaspoon black pepper
½ teaspoon onion powder
½ teaspoon garlic powder
1 egg
¼ cup (60 ml) milk
1½ cups (75 g) panko bread crumbs
4 cube steaks (4 ounces, or 115 g each)

1. Melt the butter and oil in a large skillet over medium heat; add the onion and season with salt and pepper, and then sauté the onion over medium to medium-low heat for 15 minutes until softened and browned. 2. Sprinkle the flour over the onion and stir to combine. Sauté for an additional 2 minutes until the flour smells toasty. 3. While stirring, slowly pour in the warm chicken broth and Worcestershire sauce. 4. Use the spoon to deglaze the pan by scraping up any brown bits that have accumulated on the bottom. 5. Simmer the gravy until thickened, stirring frequently to prevent scorching, 8 to 10 minutes. Taste and adjust the seasoning. 6. Keep warm over a very low flame while you make the steaks. 7. Whisk together the flour, salt, pepper, and onion and garlic powders in a shallow pie plate or dish. 8. In a second shallow dish, beat together the egg and the milk. 9. Spread the panko on a third plate or dish. 10. Dredge a cube steak in the flour, shaking off any excess. 11. Coat the steak with the egg-milk mixture. 12. Dredge the steak in the panko, shaking off any excess. Place the coated steak on a rack or plate. Repeat with the remaining steaks. 13. Place the Crisper Tray in the bottom position. Add the steak to it and close the lid. 14. Move SmartSwitch to AIR FRY/STOVETOP, set the cooking temperature to 375 degrees F and the cooking time to 14 minutes. 15. Flip the food halfway through. 16. Serve the steaks topped with onion gravy.

Per Serving: Calories 653; Fat: 27.27g; Sodium: 1233mg; Carbs: 26.9g; Fiber: 1.5g; Sugar: 3.15g; Protein: 70.56g

Simple-Spiced Pork Chops

Prep Time: 10 minutes | Cook Time: 20 minutes | Serves: 4

4 pork chops
¼ cup apple cider vinegar
1 teaspoon ground black pepper
1 teaspoon olive oil

1. Mix apple cider vinegar with olive oil and ground black pepper. Then mix pork chops with apple cider vinegar mixture. 2. Place the Crisper Tray in the bottom position. Add the food to it and close the lid. 3. Move SmartSwitch to AIR FRY/STOVETOP, set the cooking temperature to 375 degrees F and the cooking time to 20 minutes. 4. Flip the food halfway through. 5. Serve warm.

Per Serving: Calories 347; Fat: 18.53g; Sodium: 87mg; Carbs: 2.22g; Fiber: 0.2g; Sugar: 1.5g; Protein: 40.3g

Beef Empanadas

Prep Time: 20 minutes | Cook Time: 25 minutes | Serves: 4

2 tablespoons (28 g) unsalted butter
1 yellow onion, diced
1 red bell pepper, diced
1 pound (455 g) ground beef
1½ tablespoons (10.5 g) cumin
1 tablespoon (7 g) paprika
1 teaspoon oregano
1 teaspoon kosher salt, plus more for seasoning
⅓ cup (50 g) raisins
½ cup (50 g) green olives, sliced
2 hard-boiled eggs, sliced
Juice of 1 lime
1 package (12 ounces, or 340 g) frozen empanada discs, thawed
Vegetable oil for spraying

1. Heat the butter in a large, deep skillet over medium heat. 2. When the butter is foamy, add the onion, season them with salt and sauté them for 5 minutes. 3. Add the bell pepper and sauté for 3 minutes more. 4. Add the ground beef and spices and cook, stirring, until the meat is no longer pink. Remove the skillet from the heat. 5. Drain any accumulated fat from the pan. 6. Add the raisins, green olives, and eggs, stir them to combine, and allow them to cool to room temperature; add the lime juice and stir to combine. Taste and adjust the seasoning, adding more salt as necessary. 7. Remove 1 of the empanada wrappers from the package and place it on a board. Using a rolling pin, roll the wrapper out in each direction so that it is slightly larger. 8. Place a heaping ¼ cup of the beef filling on 1 side of the empanada wrapper. Moisten the edges of the wrapper with a little water and fold the wrapper in half to form a half-moon shape. Press the dough closed around the filling and then crimp the edges of the dough with a fork to seal them shut. Place the filled empanada on a baking tray lined with parchment paper. 9. Repeat with the remaining wrappers and filling. 10. Spray the empanadas with oil. 11. Place the Crisper Tray in the bottom position. Add the empanadas to it and close the lid. 12. Move SmartSwitch to AIR FRY/STOVETOP, set the cooking temperature to 375 degrees F and the cooking time to 15 minutes. 13. Flip the food after 8 minutes of cooking time. 14. You can cook the empanadas in batches. 15. Serve warm.

Per Serving: Calories 483; Fat: 26.2g; Sodium: 771mg; Carbs: 25.5g; Fiber: 1.6g; Sugar: 19.48g; Protein: 38.68g

Easy Pork Tenderloin

Prep Time: 5 minutes | Cook Time: 25 minutes | Serves: 4

2-pound pork tenderloin
1 tablespoon coconut oil, melted
1 tablespoon garlic powder
1 teaspoon dried dill

1. Rub the pork tenderloin with garlic powder and dried dill. 2. Place the Crisper Tray in the bottom position. Add the pork tenderloin to it and sprinkle with coconut oil. 3. Move SmartSwitch to AIR FRY/STOVETOP, set the cooking temperature to 390 degrees F and the cooking time to 25 minutes. 4. Serve warm.

Per Serving: Calories 363; Fat: 11.45g; Sodium: 131mg; Carbs: 2.05g; Fiber: 0.3g; Sugar: 0.06g; Protein: 59.84g

Spice-Rubbed Ribeye

Prep Time: 20 minutes | Cook Time: 10 minutes | Serves: 1-2

¾ to 1 pound (340 to 455 g) boneless ribeye, at least 1 inch (2.5 cm) thick
1½ teaspoons kosher salt
1 teaspoon brown sugar
1 teaspoon coarsely ground black pepper
½ teaspoon cumin
½ teaspoon coriander
¼ teaspoon hot paprika
Vegetable oil for spraying

1. Pat the steak dry with paper towels. Allow the steak to sit for at least 20 minutes until it is at room temperature. 2. Whisk together the salt, sugar, and spices. Rub both sides of the steak with the spice mixture. 3. Place the Crisper Tray in the bottom position. Add the steak to it and close the lid. 4. Move SmartSwitch to AIR FRY/STOVETOP, set the cooking temperature to 400 degrees F and the cooking time to 8 minutes. 5. When the cooking time is up, check the internal temperature using a meat thermometer. For medium-rare, cook to 140°F (60°C); for medium, 155°F (68°C). Continue cooking the steak until you achieve the desired doneness. 6. Allow the meat to rest for 5 minutes before slicing and serving.

Per Serving: Calories 237; Fat: 8.13g; Sodium: 1858mg; Carbs: 2.46g; Fiber: 0.5g; Sugar: 1.27g; Protein: 38.81g

Tzatziki Lamb Kofta

Prep Time: 20 minutes | Cook Time: 10 minutes | Serves: 4

1 pound (455 g) ground lamb
½ onion, grated
¼ cup (15 g) chopped fresh flat-leaf parsley, mint, or a combination
1 teaspoon kosher salt
½ teaspoon cumin
½ teaspoon coriander
½ teaspoon paprika
¼ teaspoon allspice
¼ teaspoon cinnamon
Vegetable oil for spraying
Tzatziki for serving

1. Combine the lamb, onion, herbs, salt, and spices in a medium bowl and mix thoroughly. 2. Form the lamb mixture into 8 equal, tightly packed patties. 3. Place the patties on a plate, then cover the plate and refrigerate the patties for at least 30 minutes and up to 8 hours. 4. Place the Crisper Tray in the bottom position. Add the patties to it and close the lid. 5. Move SmartSwitch to AIR FRY/STOVETOP, set the cooking temperature to 400 degrees F and the cooking time to 10 minutes. 6. Flip the patties halfway through. 7. Remove the patties to a paper towel–lined plate to absorb excess oil. 8. Serve the patties warm with Tzatziki.

Per Serving: Calories 230; Fat: 14.26g; Sodium: 655mg; Carbs: 2.21g; Fiber: 0.8g; Sugar: 0.69g; Protein: 23.67g

Crusted Pork Tenderloin with Potatoes

Prep Time: 30 minutes | Cook Time: 30 minutes | Serves: 4-6

3 tablespoons (21 g) ground cumin
1 teaspoon chili powder
1 teaspoon kosher salt
¼ teaspoon black pepper
2 cloves garlic, minced
1 pound (455 g) pork tenderloin, cut into 2 pieces
Vegetable oil for spraying
1 pound (455 g) Yukon gold potatoes, quartered
1 tablespoon (15 ml) extra-virgin olive oil

1. Combine the spices and garlic in a small bowl. Transfer 1 tablespoon of the spice mixture to another bowl and set it aside to season the potatoes. 2. Rub both pieces of the tenderloin with the remaining seasoning mixture. Set aside. 3. Place the Crisper Tray in the bottom position. Add the tenderloin pieces to it and spray them with oil. 4. Move SmartSwitch to AIR FRY/STOVETOP, set the cooking temperature to 350 degrees F and the cooking time to 20 minutes. 5. Flip the meat pieces halfway through. 6. The internal temperature of the meat pieces should reach 145 degrees F when cooked. 7. Transfer the tenderloin pieces to a platter and tent with foil to rest for 10 minutes. 8. Place the potatoes in a medium bowl. Add the reserved tablespoon of seasoning mixture and the olive oil. Toss gently to coat the potatoes. 9. AIR-FRY the potatoes in the Ninja Speedi Rapid Cooker & Air Fryer at 400 degrees F for 8 to 10 minutes until they are golden brown, tossing them halfway through. 10. Serve immediately alongside the pork tenderloin.

Per Serving: Calories 190; Fat: 4.46g; Sodium: 473mg; Carbs: 15.16g; Fiber: 2.2g; Sugar: 0.7g; Protein: 21.99g

Deconstructed Chicago Hot Dogs

Prep Time: 10 minutes | Cook Time: 7 minutes | Serves: 4

4 hot dogs
2 large dill pickles
¼ cup diced onions
1 tomato, cut into ½-inch dice
4 pickled sport peppers, diced

For Garnish (Optional):
Brown mustard
Celery salt
Poppy seeds

1. Place the Crisper Tray in the bottom position. Add the hot dogs to it and close the lid. 2. Move SmartSwitch to AIR FRY/STOVETOP, set the cooking temperature to 400 degrees F and the cooking time to 7 minutes. 3. Quarter one of the dill pickles lengthwise, so that you have 4 pickle spears. Finely dice the other pickle. 4. Transfer the cooked hot dogs to a serving platter and arrange them in a row, alternating with the pickle spears. Top them with the diced pickles, onions, tomato, and sport peppers. Drizzle brown mustard on top and garnish with celery salt and poppy seeds, if desired. 5. Serve warm. You can store the leftovers in an airtight container in the refrigerator for up to 3 days.

Per Serving: Calories 424; Fat: 35.76g; Sodium: 1387mg; Carbs: 8.17g; Fiber: 1.7g; Sugar: 3.32g; Protein: 17.74g

Glazed Baby Back Ribs

Prep Time: 30 minutes | Cook Time: 60 minutes | Serves: 4

- 1 teaspoon Chinese five-spice powder
- ½ teaspoon garlic powder
- 1 teaspoon kosher salt
- 1 teaspoon black pepper
- 2½ to 3 pounds (1 to 1⅓ kg) rack baby back ribs, cut into 4 pieces
- ¼ cup (60 ml) soy sauce, preferably low-sodium
- 1 tablespoon (9.5 g) brown sugar
- 1 tablespoon (15 ml) vegetable oil
- ½ tablespoon (4 g) grated fresh ginger
- 1 clove garlic, minced
- 3 teaspoons rice vinegar
- 1 teaspoon toasted sesame oil

1. Combine the Chinese five-spice powder, garlic powder, salt, and pepper in a small bowl and whisk to combine. 2. Place each rib section on a large piece of foil and sprinkle all over with the spice mixture. Wrap the foil tightly around each rib section. 3. Place the Crisper Tray in the bottom position. Add the ribs to it and close the lid. 4. Move SmartSwitch to AIR FRY/STOVETOP, set the cooking temperature to 250 degrees F and the cooking time to 50 minutes. 5. While the ribs are cooking, combine the soy sauce, brown sugar, oil, ginger, garlic, rice vinegar, and sesame oil in a small bowl and whisk until combined. 6. Remove the cooked ribs to a rimmed baking sheet. Allow the ribs to cool slightly before removing the foil. 7. Brush the ribs evenly with the sauce mixture and then return to the pot. 8. AIR-FRY the ribs at 400 degrees F for 10 minutes more, occasionally basting the ribs with additional sauce. 9. The ribs should be crispy, tender, and slightly charred when cooked. 10. Brush the cooked ribs with any remaining sauce and serve immediately.

Per Serving: Calories 727; Fat: 52.05g; Sodium: 991mg; Carbs: 7.77g; Fiber: 0.6g; Sugar: 5.09g; Protein: 57.25g

Butter Pork Tenderloin Chopps

Prep Time: 5 minutes | Cook Time: 30 minutes | Serves: 4

- 2-pound pork tenderloin, chopped
- ¼ cup butter
- 1 teaspoon chili powder
- ½ teaspoon salt

1. Gently mix all of the ingredients. 2. Place the Crisper Tray in the bottom position. Add the food to it and close the lid. 3. Move SmartSwitch to AIR FRY/STOVETOP, set the cooking temperature to 390 degrees F and the cooking time to 30 minutes. 4. Serve and enjoy.

Per Serving: Calories 428; Fat: 19.57g; Sodium: 531mg; Carbs: 0.34g; Fiber: 0.2g; Sugar: 0.06g; Protein: 59.57g

Savory Pork Shoulder

Prep Time: 20 minutes | Cook Time: 40 minutes | Serves: 5

3-pound pork shoulder
1 tablespoon cream cheese
1 tablespoon avocado oil
1 tablespoon lemon juice
½ teaspoon salt
½ tablespoon cayenne pepper

1. Mix cream cheese with avocado oil, lemon juice, salt, and cayenne pepper in a shallow bowl. 2. Carefully rub the pork shoulder with cream cheese mixture and leave for 15 minutes to marinate. Then sprinkle the pork shoulder with avocado oil. 3. Place the Crisper Tray in the bottom position. Add the pork shoulder to it and close the lid. 4. Move SmartSwitch to AIR FRY/STOVETOP, set the cooking temperature to 360 degrees F and the cooking time to 40 minutes. 5. Serve warm.

Per Serving: Calories 763; Fat: 51.9g; Sodium: 404mg; Carbs: 0.62g; Fiber: 0.2g; Sugar: 0.24g; Protein: 68.52g

Pecan Pork Stuffing

Prep Time: 10 minutes | Cook Time: 35 minutes | Serves: 6

4 oz. pork rinds
2 pecans, chopped
1 teaspoon Italian seasonings
½ teaspoon white pepper
1 egg, beaten
4 tablespoons almond flour
3 cups ground pork
1 tablespoon avocado oil
¼ cup heavy cream

1. Put all ingredients in the mixing bowl and stir until homogenous. 2. Place the Crisper Tray in the bottom position. Add the mixture to it and close the lid. 3. Move SmartSwitch to AIR FRY/STOVETOP, set the cooking temperature to 360 degrees F and the cooking time to 35 minutes. 4. Stir the mixture every 10 minutes during cooking. 5. Serve warm.

Per Serving: Calories 570; Fat: 50.33g; Sodium: 112mg; Carbs: 5.93g; Fiber: 3.7g; Sugar: 1.78g; Protein: 23.23g

Mustard Pork Chops

Prep Time: 10 minutes | Cook Time: 20 minutes | Serves: 4

4 pork chops
1 tablespoon Dijon mustard
1 teaspoon chili powder
1 tablespoon avocado oil

1. Mix the Dijon mustard, chili powder and avocado oil. 2. Carefully brush the pork chops with the mustard mixture from both sides. 3. Place the Crisper Tray in the bottom position. Add the pork chops to it and close the lid. 4. Move SmartSwitch to AIR FRY/STOVETOP, set the cooking temperature to 375 degrees F and the cooking time to 20 minutes. 5. Flip the food halfway through. 6. Serve warm.

Per Serving: Calories 363; Fat: 21.09g; Sodium: 149mg; Carbs: 0.56g; Fiber: 0.4g; Sugar: 0.08g; Protein: 40.44g

African Pork Shoulder

Prep Time: 15 minutes | Cook Time: 50 minutes | Serves: 4

2-pound pork shoulder
1 teaspoon dried sage
1 teaspoon curry powder
¼ cup plain yogurt
1 tablespoon avocado oil

1. Mix curry powder with plain yogurt and avocado oil; add dried sage and stir the mixture. 2. Brush the pork shoulder with plain yogurt mixture and leave for 20 minutes to marinate. 3. Place the Crisper Tray in the bottom position. Add the pork shoulder and all the remaining yogurt mixture to it and close the lid. 4. Move SmartSwitch to AIR FRY/STOVETOP, set the cooking temperature to 365 degrees F and the cooking time to 50 minutes. 5. Serve warm.

Per Serving: Calories 648; Fat: 44.21g; Sodium: 139mg; Carbs: 1.1g; Fiber: 0.3g; Sugar: 0.73g; Protein: 57.48g

Bacon Cheeseburger Casserole

Prep Time: 20 minutes | Cook Time: 55 minutes | Serves: 4

¼ pound reduced-sodium bacon
1 pound 85% lean ground beef
1 clove garlic, minced
¼ teaspoon onion powder
4 eggs
¼ cup heavy cream
¼ cup tomato paste
2 tablespoons dill pickle relish
¼ teaspoon salt
¼ teaspoon freshly ground black pepper
1½ cups grated Cheddar cheese, divided

1. Place the Crisper Tray in the bottom position. Add the bacon to it in a single layer and close the lid. 2. Move SmartSwitch to AIR FRY/STOVETOP, set the cooking temperature to 350 degrees F and the cooking time to 10 minutes. 3. Check for crispiness and air fry for 2 to 3 minutes longer if needed. Transfer the bacon to a plate lined with paper towels and let cool. Drain the grease. 4. Crumble the beef into a single layer in the pot and sprinkle with the onion powder; air-fry the beef for 15 to 20 minutes until browned. 5. Whisk the eggs, cream, tomato paste, pickle relish, salt, and pepper in a bowl. Stir in 1 cup of the cheese. Set aside. 6. Lightly coat a 6-cup casserole dish that will fit in air fryer with olive oil. Transfer the cooked beef to the dish, breaking up any large pieces of beef. Drain the grease. 7. Crumble the bacon and add it to the beef, spreading the meats into an even layer. Pour the egg mixture over the beef mixture and top with the remaining ½ cup of cheese. 8. Cook the food at 350 degrees F for 20 to 25 minutes until the eggs are set and the top is golden brown. 9. Serve warm.

Per Serving: Calories 740; Fat: 53g; Sodium: 842mg; Carbs: 8.33g; Fiber: 0.8g; Sugar: 5.45g; Protein: 55.58g

Pork Milanese

Prep Time: 10 minutes | Cook Time: 15 minutes | Serves: 4

4 (1-inch) boneless pork chops
Fine sea salt and ground black pepper
2 large eggs
¾ cup powdered Parmesan cheese (about 2¼ ounces) (or pork dust for dairy-free)
Chopped fresh parsley, for garnish
Lemon slices, for serving

1. Place the pork chops between 2 sheets of plastic wrap and pound them with the flat side of a meat tenderizer until they're ¼ inch thick. 2. Lightly season both sides of the chops with salt and pepper. 3. Lightly beat the eggs in a shallow bowl. Divide the Parmesan cheese evenly between 2 bowls and set the bowls in this order: Parmesan, eggs, Parmesan. Dredge a chop in the first bowl of Parmesan, then dip it in the eggs, and then dredge it again in the second bowl of Parmesan, making sure both sides and all edges are well coated. 4. Repeat with the remaining chops. 5. Place the Crisper Tray in the bottom position. Add the chops to it and close the lid. 6. Move SmartSwitch to AIR FRY/STOVETOP, set the cooking temperature to 400 degrees F and the cooking time to 12 minutes. 7. Flip the food halfway through. 8. Garnish the dish with fresh parsley and serve immediately with lemon slices. 9. You can store the leftovers in an airtight container in the refrigerator for up to 3 days.

Per Serving: Calories 354; Fat: 13.97g; Sodium: 442mg; Carbs: 5.76g; Fiber: 0.7g; Sugar: 1.06g; Protein: 48.85g

Sausages with Peppers and Onions

Prep Time: 5 minutes | Cook Time: 30 minutes | Serves: 3

- 1 medium onion, thinly sliced
- 1 yellow or orange bell pepper, thinly sliced
- 1 red bell pepper, thinly sliced
- ¼ cup avocado oil or melted coconut oil
- 1 teaspoon fine sea salt
- 6 Italian sausages
- Dijon mustard, for serving (optional)

1. Place the onion and peppers in a large bowl. Drizzle with the oil and toss well to coat the veggies. Season them with the salt. 2. Place the Crisper Tray in the bottom position. Add the onion and peppers to it and close the lid. 3. Move SmartSwitch to AIR FRY/STOVETOP, set the cooking temperature to 400 degrees F and the cooking time to 8 minutes. Stir them halfway through. 4. Set aside when cooked. 5. AIR-FRY the sausages at 400 degrees F for 20 minutes until they are crispy and golden brown. 6. During the last minute or two of cooking, add the onion and peppers with the sausages to warm them through. 7. Place the onion and peppers on a serving platter and arrange the sausages on top. Serve Dijon mustard on the side, if desired. 8. Store leftovers in an airtight container in the fridge for up to 7 days or in the freezer for up to a month.

Per Serving: Calories 576; Fat: 53.77g; Sodium: 1604mg; Carbs: 6.25g; Fiber: 0.8g; Sugar: 0.92g; Protein: 17.04g

Healthy Scotch Eggs

Prep Time: 10 minutes | Cook Time: 15 minutes | Serves: 8

- 2 pounds ground pork or ground beef
- 2 teaspoons fine sea salt
- ½ teaspoon ground black pepper, plus more for garnish
- 8 large hard-boiled eggs, peeled
- 2 cups pork dust
- Dijon mustard, for serving (optional)

1. Place the ground pork in a large bowl, add the salt and pepper, and use your hands to mix until seasoned throughout. Flatten about ¼ pound of ground pork in the palm of your hand and place a peeled egg in the center. Fold the pork completely around the egg. 2. Repeat with the remaining eggs. 3. Place the pork dust in a medium-sized bowl. One at a time, roll the ground pork–covered eggs in the pork dust and use your hands to press it into the eggs to form a nice crust. 4. Place the Crisper Tray in the bottom position. Add the eggs to it and spray them with avocado oil. 5. Move SmartSwitch to AIR FRY/STOVETOP, set the cooking temperature to 400 degrees F and the cooking time to 15 minutes. 6. When cooked, the internal temperature of the pork should reach 145 degrees F and the outside should be golden brown. 7. Garnish the dish with ground black pepper and serve with Dijon mustard, if desired. 8. Store leftovers in an airtight container in the fridge for up to 7 days or in the freezer for up to a month.

Per Serving: Calories 583; Fat: 48.35g; Sodium: 1716mg; Carbs: 3.77g; Fiber: 0g; Sugar: 0.56g; Protein: 30.94g

Savory Sausage Cobbler

Prep Time: 15 minutes | Cook Time: 35 minutes | Serves: 4

Filling:

1 pound ground Italian sausage
1 cup sliced mushrooms
1 teaspoon fine sea salt
2 cups marinara sauce

Biscuits:

3 large egg whites
¾ cup blanched almond flour
1 teaspoon baking powder
¼ teaspoon fine sea salt
2½ tablespoons very cold unsalted butter, cut into ¼-inch pieces
Fresh basil leaves, for garnish

1. Place the sausage in a suitable pie pan. Break up the sausage and spread it evenly on the bottom of the pan. 2. Place the Crisper Tray in the bottom position. Place the pan on the tray and close the lid. 3. Move SmartSwitch to AIR FRY/STOVETOP, and then use the center front arrows to select BAKE/ROAST. Set the cooking temperature to 400 degrees F and the cooking time to 5 minutes. 4. When cooked, use a fork or metal spatula to crumble the sausage more. 5. Season the mushrooms with the salt and add them to the pie pan. Stir to combine the mushrooms and sausage. 6. Resume cooking the food for 4 minutes more until the mushrooms are soft. 7. Add the marinara sauce to the cooked dish and stir well. Set aside. 8. Place the egg whites in a large mixing bowl or the bowl of a stand mixer. Using a hand mixer or stand mixer, whip the egg whites until stiff peaks form. 9. In a medium-sized bowl, whisk together the almond flour, baking powder, and salt, and then cut in the butter. 10. Gently fold the flour mixture into the egg whites with a rubber spatula. 11. Using a large spoon or ice cream scoop, spoon one-quarter of the dough on top of the sausage mixture, making sure the butter stays in separate clumps. 12. Repeat with the remaining dough, spacing the biscuits about 1 inch apart. 13. BAKE the biscuits at 400 degrees F for 5 minutes, and then lower the heat to 325°F and cook for another 15 to 20 minutes, until the biscuits are golden brown. 14. Serve garnished with fresh basil leaves. 15. Store leftovers in an airtight container in the refrigerator for up to 3 days.

Per Serving: Calories 698; Fat: 58.25g; Sodium: 2659mg; Carbs: 20.09g; Fiber: 5.2g; Sugar: 6.9g; Protein: 27.35g

Pork Chops with Scallions

Prep Time: 25 minutes | Cook Time: 20 minutes | Serves: 4

2 tablespoons avocado oil
4 pork chops
2 oz. scallions, minced
1 teaspoon onion powder

1. Mix avocado oil with minced scallions and onion powder in a shallow bowl. 2. Mix scallions mixture with pork chops and leave for 10 to15 minutes to marinate. 3. Place the Crisper Tray in the bottom position. Add the pork chops to it and close the lid. 4. Move SmartSwitch to AIR FRY/STOVETOP, set the cooking temperature to 380 degrees F and the cooking time to 20 minutes. 5. Flip the food halfway through. 6. Serve warm.

Per Serving: Calories 397; Fat: 24.4g; Sodium: 89mg; Carbs: 1.52g; Fiber: 0.5g; Sugar: 0.37g; Protein: 40.53g

Onion & Beef Stuffed Peppers

Prep Time: 20 minutes | Cook Time: 50 minutes | Serves: 4

1 pound 85% lean ground beef
½ yellow onion, chopped
4 bell peppers, tops and seeds removed
1 (10-ounce) package cauliflower "rice," fresh or frozen
½ cup tomato sauce
2 tablespoons chopped fresh parsley
1 teaspoon salt
½ teaspoon freshly ground black pepper
1 cup shredded Cheddar cheese
1 teaspoon fresh chopped dill or parsley, for garnish (optional)

1. Place the Crisper Tray in the bottom position. Crumble the beef into a single layer in the pot, and scatter the onion on top. 2. Move SmartSwitch to AIR FRY/STOVETOP, set the cooking temperature to 360 degrees F and the cooking time to 20 minutes. 3. Arrange the bell peppers in a microwave-safe dish and cover loosely with parchment paper or plastic wrap. Microwave on high for 2 to 3 minutes until the peppers begin to soften. 4. To assemble the peppers, carefully transfer the beef and onions to a large mixing bowl. Use the side of a spoon to break up any large pieces of beef. Drain the grease and wash the pot. 5. To the beef mixture add the cauliflower "rice," tomato sauce, parsley, salt, and black pepper. Stir gently until thoroughly combined. 6. Divide the mixture among the peppers and arrange cut-side up in the air fryer basket. Air-fry them for 15 to 20 minutes until the peppers are soft. Top the dish with the cheese and air fry for 1 to 2 minutes longer until melted. 7. Garnish the dish with herbs if desired.

Per Serving: Calories 463; Fat: 25.33g; Sodium: 1342mg; Carbs: 15.93g; Fiber: 4.6g; Sugar: 8.05g; Protein: 8.05g

Steak Salad with Blue Cheese Dressing

Prep Time: 20 minutes | Cook Time: 15 minutes | Serves: 4

1 pound sirloin steak
1 tablespoon steak seasoning
8 cups chopped romaine lettuce
2 avocados, peeled, pitted, and sliced
½ cup cherry tomatoes, halved
¼ red onion, thinly sliced
¼ cup crumbled blue cheese

Smoky Blue Cheese Dressing

½ cup mayonnaise
¼ cup buttermilk
1 tablespoon chipotle hot sauce
1 teaspoon garlic powder
½ teaspoon Worcestershire sauce
¼ cup crumbled blue cheese
Salt and freshly ground black pepper

1. Rub the steak with the steak seasoning. 2. Place the Crisper Tray in the bottom position. Add the steak to it and spray with olive oil. 3. Move SmartSwitch to AIR FRY/STOVETOP, set the cooking temperature to 400 degrees F and the cooking time to 15 minutes. 4. Flip the steak halfway through. 5. Cook the steak until a thermometer inserted into the thickest part indicates the desired doneness, 125 degrees F (rare) or 150 degrees F (medium). 6. Let the steaks rest for 10 minutes before slicing into bite-size pieces. 7. In a bowl, combine the mayonnaise, buttermilk, hot sauce, garlic powder, and Worcestershire sauce until smooth. Stir in the blue cheese and season to taste with salt and freshly ground black pepper. 8. Place the lettuce on the bottom of the plate or serving bowl. Top them with the avocado slices, tomatoes, and red onion, followed by the steak slices. 9. Scatter the blue cheese crumbles on top and serve with the dressing on the side.

Per Serving: Calories 479; Fat: 32.53g; Sodium: 818mg; Carbs: 16.9g; Fiber: 9.7g; Sugar: 3.65g; Protein: 32.37g

Lamb Kofta with Yogurt Sauce

Prep Time: 40 minutes | Cook Time: 10 minutes | Serves: 6

For the kofta

1 pound ground lamb	cinnamon
¼ cup fresh parsley, roughly chopped	¼ teaspoon ground allspice
2 garlic cloves, minced	¼ teaspoon cayenne pepper
¼ white onion, diced	
1 teaspoon salt	¼ teaspoon ground ginger
1 teaspoon ground cumin	3 tablespoons olive oil, divided
½ teaspoon black pepper	
¼ teaspoon ground	

For the mint-yogurt sauce

1 cup nonfat plain Greek yogurt	½ teaspoon ground cumin
½ cup fresh mint, chopped	¼ teaspoon cayenne pepper
1 garlic clove, minced	¼ teaspoon salt
2 tablespoons lemon juice	¼ teaspoon black pepper

1. In a large bowl, combine the ground lamb with the parsley, garlic, onion, and all the spices and 2 tablespoons olive oil, then mix until well combined and the spices are distributed evenly. 2. Divide the mixture into 4 equal quantities, and roll each into a long oval. 3. Brush the remaining 1 tablespoon of olive oil over the lamb ovals. 4. Place the Crisper Tray in the bottom position. Add the food to it and close the lid. 5. Move SmartSwitch to AIR FRY/STOVETOP, set the cooking temperature to 360 degrees F and the cooking time to 10 minutes. 6. The internal temperature should reach 145°F when cooked. 7. Mix the ingredients for the yogurt sauce and set aside. 8. Serve each kofta with a generous serving of mint sauce for dipping.

Per Serving: Calories 266; Fat: 17.94g; Sodium: 552mg; Carbs: 3.57g; Fiber: 0.5g; Sugar: 1.65g; Protein: 22.98g

Beef Tips with Onions

Prep Time: 5 minutes | Cook Time: 10 minutes | Serves: 4

1 pound rib eye steak, cubed	oregano
	1 teaspoon salt
2 garlic cloves, minced	½ teaspoon black pepper
2 tablespoons olive oil	1 yellow onion, thinly sliced
1 tablespoon fresh	

1. In a medium bowl, combine the steak, garlic, olive oil, oregano, salt, pepper, and onion. Mix them until all of the beef and onion are well coated. 2. Place the Crisper Tray in the bottom position. Place the food on the tray and close the lid. 3. Move SmartSwitch to AIR FRY/STOVETOP, and then use the center front arrows to select BAKE/ROAST. Set the cooking temperature to 380 degrees F and the cooking time to 10 minutes. 4. Stir the mixture halfway through. 5. Let the dish rest for 5 minutes before serving with some favorite sides.

Per Serving: Calories 366; Fat: 30.58g; Sodium: 647mg; Carbs: 2.68g; Fiber: 0.6g; Sugar: 0.78g; Protein: 20.69g

Lebanese Malfouf

Prep Time: 15 minutes | **Cook Time:** 35 minutes | **Serves:** 4

- 1 head green cabbage
- 1 pound lean ground beef
- ½ cup long-grain brown rice
- 4 garlic cloves, minced
- 1 teaspoon salt
- ½ teaspoon black pepper
- 1 teaspoon ground cinnamon
- 2 tablespoons chopped fresh mint
- Juice of 1 lemon
- Olive oil cooking spray
- ½ cup beef broth
- 1 tablespoon olive oil

1. Cut the cabbage in half and remove the core. Remove 12 of the larger leaves to use for the cabbage rolls. 2. Bring a large pot of salted water to a boil, then drop the cabbage leaves into the water, boiling them for 3 minutes. Remove from the water and set aside. 3. In a large bowl, combine the ground beef, rice, garlic, salt, pepper, cinnamon, mint, and lemon juice, and mix together until combined. Divide this mixture into 12 equal portions. 4. Lightly coat a small casserole dish with olive oil cooking spray. 5. Place a cabbage leaf on a clean work surface. Place a spoonful of the beef mixture on one side of the leaf, leaving space on all other sides. Fold the two perpendicular sides inward and then roll forward, tucking tightly as rolled. 6. Place the finished rolls into the baking dish, stacking them on top of each other if needed. 7. Pour the beef broth over the top of the cabbage rolls so that it soaks down between them, and then brush the tops with the olive oil. 8. BAKE the dish at 360 degrees F for 30 minutes. 9. Serve warm.

Per Serving: Calories 546; Fat: 25.58g; Sodium: 751mg; Carbs: 23.35g; Fiber: 1.5g; Sugar: 0.69g; Protein: 52.68g

Cheese Beef Stuffed Peppers

Prep Time: 10 minutes | **Cook Time:** 30 minutes | **Serves:** 4

- 1 pound lean ground beef
- ½ cup cooked brown rice
- 2 Roma tomatoes, diced
- 3 garlic cloves, minced
- ½ yellow onion, diced
- 2 tablespoons fresh oregano, chopped
- 1 teaspoon salt
- ½ teaspoon black pepper
- ¼ teaspoon ground allspice
- 2 bell peppers, halved and seeded
- 4 ounces goat cheese
- ¼ cup fresh parsley, chopped

1. In a large bowl, combine the ground beef, rice, tomatoes, garlic, onion, oregano, salt, pepper, and allspice. 2. Divide the beef mixture equally into the halved bell peppers and top each with about 1 ounce of the goat cheese. 3. Place the Crisper Tray in the bottom position. Add the peppers to it and close the lid. 4. Move SmartSwitch to AIR FRY/STOVETOP, and then use the center front arrows to select BAKE/ROAST. Set the cooking temperature to 360 degrees F and the cooking time to 30 minutes. 5. Remove the peppers and top with fresh parsley before serving.

Per Serving: Calories 432; Fat: 23.18g; Sodium: 780mg; Carbs: 13.95g; Fiber: 2.4g; Sugar: 4.14g; Protein: 40.99g

Chapter 6 Seafood Recipes

Shrimp Caesar Salad 76

Homemade Fish 'n' Chips 76

Chili-Lime Tilapia 77

Cilantro Butter Mahi Mahi 77

Shrimp with Orange Sauce 78

Shrimp with Wild Rice Pilaf 78

Caper Salmon Burgers 79

Cod Piccata with Potatoes 79

Salmon with Tomatoes and Green Beans 80

Lemo Tuna Steaks 80

Flavorful Flounder au Gratin 81

Haddock Fish Fingers 81

Salmon with Tomatoes and Olives 82

Parmesan Perch 82

Sea Bass with Root Vegetables 83

Shrimp Pita 83

Lemon-Pepper Trout Fillets 84

Shrimp Caesar Salad

Prep Time: 15 minutes | Cook Time: 25 minutes | Serves: 4

- 1 large lemon
- 1 pound shelled, deveined, large (20–24 count) shrimp
- 1 tablespoon olive oil
- 3 garlic cloves, crushed with press
- 1 teaspoon hot paprika
- ⅜ teaspoon salt
- Oil in mister
- 1 head romaine lettuce
- 1 head radicchio
- ¼ cup plain nonfat Greek yogurt
- 3 tablespoons finely grated Parmesan cheese
- 1 teaspoon Dijon mustard
- ¼ teaspoon pepper
- 1 cup prepared unseasoned croutons

1. From lemon, grate 1 teaspoon zest and squeeze 3 tablespoons juice. 2. In a large bowl, toss shrimp, olive oil, 2 crushed garlic cloves, hot paprika, lemon zest, and ⅛ teaspoon salt. 3. Place the Crisper Tray in the bottom position. Add the shrimp to it and close the lid. 4. Move SmartSwitch to AIR FRY/STOVETOP, set the cooking temperature to 400 degrees F and the cooking time to 3 minutes. 5. Thinly slice romaine lettuce and radicchio, and place the greens in a large serving bowl. 6. In a small bowl, whisk Greek yogurt, Parmesan cheese, mustard, 1 crushed garlic clove, lemon juice, and ¼ teaspoon each salt and pepper. Toss with lettuce mixture in bowl. 7. Top the salad with shrimp and croutons. Enjoy.

Per Serving: Calories 504; Fat: 6.39g; Sodium: 396mg; Carbs: 85.88g; Fiber: 25.6g; Sugar: 12.52g; Protein: 30.06g

Homemade Fish 'n' Chips

Prep Time: 10 minutes | Cook Time: 15 minutes | Serves: 4

- 1½ pounds cod fillets, cut into strips
- 3 large egg whites, beaten
- 6 ounces salt-and-vinegar potato chips, finely crushed
- ½ teaspoon salt
- 1 pound frozen peas
- 3 tablespoons butter
- 1 tablespoon lemon juice
- ¼ teaspoon pepper
- Lemon wedges and chives, for serving

1. Cut fish into equal-size pieces; fold thinner tail ends in half, if needed, and secure with a toothpick. Dip cod into egg white, then chips. 2. Place the Crisper Tray in the bottom position. Add the fish to it and close the lid. 3. Move SmartSwitch to AIR FRY/STOVETOP, set the cooking temperature to 350 degrees F and the cooking time to 10 minutes. 4. Sprinkle the fish with ¼ teaspoon salt. 5. Microwave on High frozen peas, butter, lemon juice, and ¼ teaspoon each salt and pepper for 5 minutes. Puree them in food processor. 6. Serve fish with pea puree, lemon wedges, and chives.

Per Serving: Calories 463; Fat: 18.46g; Sodium: 924mg; Carbs: 38.11g; Fiber: 5.6g; Sugar: 5.05g; Protein: 35.03g

Chili-Lime Tilapia

Prep Time: 5 minutes | Cook Time: 8 minutes | Serves: 4

- ½ teaspoon salt
- ½ teaspoon freshly ground black pepper
- ¼ teaspoon garlic powder
- ¼ teaspoon chili powder
- ¼ teaspoon smoked paprika
- 4 (4-ounce) tilapia fillets
- 2 tablespoons freshly squeezed lime juice

1. In a small bowl, mix together the salt, pepper, garlic powder, chili powder, and paprika. 2. Place the fish fillets in a shallow bowl. Pour the lime juice over the fillets and then sprinkle it with the spice blend, making sure to coat all sides well. 3. Place the Crisper Tray in the bottom position. Add the fish to it and close the lid. 4. Move SmartSwitch to AIR FRY/STOVETOP, set the cooking temperature to 400 degrees F and the cooking time to 9 minutes. 5. Flip the fish halfway through. 6. The fish should be crispy when cooked. 7. Serve warm.

Per Serving: Calories 116; Fat: 2.03g; Sodium: 356mg; Carbs: 1.14g; Fiber: 0.2g; Sugar: 0.16g; Protein: 23.43g

Cilantro Butter Mahi Mahi

Prep Time: 5 minutes | Cook Time: 15 minutes | Serves: 4

- 2 tablespoons butter, melted
- 2 tablespoons chopped fresh cilantro
- 2 garlic cloves, minced
- ½ teaspoon salt
- ¼ teaspoon freshly ground black pepper
- ¼ teaspoon chili powder
- 4 (4-ounce) boneless, skinless mahi mahi fillets

1. In a small bowl, mix together the butter, cilantro, garlic, salt, pepper, and chili powder. 2. Place the mahi mahi fillets on a large plate. Spread the butter mixture over the top of the fillets. 3. Place the Crisper Tray in the bottom position. Add the fillets to it and close the lid. 4. Move SmartSwitch to AIR FRY/STOVETOP, set the cooking temperature to 375 degrees F and the cooking time to 12 minutes. 5. Flip the fillets halfway through. 6. Serve warm.

Per Serving: Calories 251; Fat: 12.25g; Sodium: 645mg; Carbs: 24.39g; Fiber: 1.8g; Sugar: 6.12g; Protein: 10.72g

Shrimp with Orange Sauce

Prep Time: 15 minutes | Cook Time: 15 minutes | Serves: 4

½ cup unsweetened grated coconut
¼ cup whole-wheat bread crumbs
¼ cup whole-wheat flour
¼ teaspoon smoked paprika
¼ teaspoon freshly ground black pepper
¼ teaspoon salt
1 egg
1 teaspoon water
1 pound medium shrimp, peeled and deveined
Extra-virgin olive oil, in a spray bottle, for greasing
2 tablespoons maple syrup
½ teaspoon rice vinegar
⅛ teaspoon red pepper flakes
¼ cup freshly squeezed orange juice
1 teaspoon cornstarch

1. In a shallow bowl, mix together the coconut, bread crumbs, flour, paprika, black pepper, and salt. 2. In a separate shallow bowl, whisk together the egg and water. 3. Dip a shrimp into the egg, shaking off any excess. Dip it into the coconut–bread crumb mixture, making sure to coat it completely. Repeat with the rest of the shrimp. 4. Place the Crisper Tray in the bottom position. Add the shrimp to it and close the lid. 5. Move SmartSwitch to AIR FRY/STOVETOP, set the cooking temperature to 350 degrees F and the cooking time to 8 minutes. Flip the shrimp after 5 minutes of cooking time. 6. In a small saucepan, combine the maple syrup, vinegar, and red pepper flakes and stir until combined. 7. In a small bowl, mix together the orange juice and cornstarch. Add it to the saucepan, and bring to a boil over medium heat. Cook and stir them for 5 minutes or until reduced and beginning to thicken. 8. Let the food sit for 5 minutes before serving

Substitution Tip: Instead of orange sauce, serve with clean tartar sauce or cocktail sauce.

Per Serving: Calories 209; Fat: 4.32g; Sodium: 906mg; Carbs: 22.12g; Fiber: 1.6g; Sugar: 8.83g; Protein: 19.97g

Shrimp with Wild Rice Pilaf

Prep Time: 5 minutes | Cook Time: 5 minutes | Serves: 4

1 pound medium shrimp, peeled and deveined
¼ cup pesto sauce
1 lemon, sliced
2 cups cooked wild rice pilaf

1. In a medium bowl, toss the shrimp with the pesto sauce until well coated. 2. Place the Crisper Tray in the bottom position. Add the shrimp and lemon slices to it and close the lid. 3. ROAST the shrimp at 360 degrees F for 5 minutes. 4. Remove the lemons and discard. Serve a quarter of the shrimp over ½ cup wild rice with some favorite steamed vegetables.

Per Serving: Calories 532; Fat: 11.08g; Sodium: 2112mg; Carbs: 80.39g; Fiber: 1.4g; Sugar: 1.99g; Protein: 27.63g

Caper Salmon Burgers

Prep Time: 15 minutes | Cook Time: 12 minutes | Serves: 4

- 1 pound boneless, skinless salmon fillet
- 1 scallion, both white and green parts, diced
- 2 tablespoons Primal Kitchen mayonnaise or other clean mayonnaise, plus more for serving
- 1 egg
- 1 teaspoon capers, drained
- ½ teaspoon salt
- ½ teaspoon freshly ground black pepper
- ¼ teaspoon paprika
- Zest of 1 lemon
- ¼ cup whole-wheat bread crumbs
- 4 whole-wheat buns, toasted
- 4 teaspoons whole-grain mustard
- 4 lettuce leaves
- 1 small tomato, sliced

1. Cut the salmon in half. Cut one half into chunks and place them into a food processor. Add the scallion, mayonnaise, egg, capers, salt, pepper, paprika, and lemon zest and pulse until the salmon is pureed. 2. Dice the remaining half of salmon into ¼-inch pieces. 3. In a large bowl, combine the salmon pieces, pureed salmon, and bread crumbs and stir until combined. 4. Form the mixture into 4 patties. 5. Place the Crisper Tray in the bottom position. Add the patties to it and close the lid. 6. Move SmartSwitch to AIR FRY/STOVETOP, set the cooking temperature to 400 degrees F and the cooking time to 12 minutes. Flip the patties halfway through. 7. Serve the salmon burgers on the whole-wheat buns with a teaspoon of mustard, more mayonnaise, lettuce, and a slice of tomato.

Per Serving: Calories 371; Fat: 12.53g; Sodium: 904mg; Carbs: 48.19g; Fiber: 4.8g; Sugar: 7.55g

Cod Piccata with Potatoes

Prep Time: 15 minutes | Cook Time: 15 minutes | Serves: 4

- 4 (4-ounce) cod fillets
- 1 tablespoon unsalted butter
- 2 teaspoons capers, drained
- 1 garlic clove, minced
- 2 tablespoons freshly squeezed lemon juice
- ½ pound asparagus, trimmed
- 2 large potatoes, cubed
- 1 tablespoon extra-virgin olive oil
- ¼ teaspoon salt
- ¼ teaspoon garlic powder
- ¼ teaspoon freshly ground black pepper

1. Place the cod fillets on a large piece of aluminum foil. Add the butter, capers, garlic, and lemon juice over the cod and wrap up the foil to enclose the fish in a pouch. 2. In a large bowl, toss together the asparagus, potatoes, olive oil, salt, garlic powder, and pepper. 3. Place the Crisper Tray in the bottom position. Add the potatoes and asparagus to it and close the lid. 4. Move SmartSwitch to AIR FRY/STOVETOP, set the cooking temperature to 380 degrees F and the cooking time to 12 minutes. 5. Stir the food and carefully place the foil packet of fish on top of the vegetables after 4 minutes of cooking time. 6. Let the dish rest for 5 minutes before serving.

Per Serving: Calories 269; Fat: 4.2g; Sodium: 642mg; Carbs: 35.66g; Fiber: 5.5g; Sugar: 2.73g; Protein: 23.04g

Salmon with Tomatoes and Green Beans

Prep Time: 5 minutes | Cook Time: 15 minutes | Serves: 4

- 4 tablespoons (½ stick) unsalted butter
- 4 garlic cloves, minced
- ¼ cup chopped fresh dill
- ½ teaspoon salt
- ½ teaspoon freshly ground black pepper
- 4 (4-ounce) wild-caught salmon fillets, skin removed
- 1 lemon, thinly sliced
- 1 pound green beans, trimmed
- 1 cup halved cherry tomatoes

1. In a small bowl, mix together the butter, garlic, dill, salt, and pepper. 2. Place the salmon fillets on a large plate and spread the butter mixture over them. 3. Place the Crisper Tray in the bottom position. Add the salmon to it and place about three-quarters of the lemon slices on top of the fillets. Place the green beans and tomatoes around the fillets. 4. Move SmartSwitch to AIR FRY/STOVETOP, set the cooking temperature to 390 degrees F and the cooking time to 15 minutes. 5. Serve the filletswith the remaining lemon slices.

Per Serving: Calories 304; Fat: 15.01g; Sodium: 741mg; Carbs: 12.4g; Fiber: 3g; Sugar: 5.85g; Protein: 32.34g

Lemo Tuna Steaks

Prep Time: 20 minutes | Cook Time: 7 minutes | Serves: 4

- ½ tablespoon extra-virgin olive oil
- 1 garlic clove, minced
- ¼ teaspoon salt
- ¼ teaspoon chili powder
- 1 tablespoon plus 1 teaspoon freshly squeezed lemon juice
- 1 tablespoon chopped fresh cilantro
- 4 (4-ounce) tuna steaks, about 1 inch thick
- 1 lemon, thinly sliced

1. In a wide, shallow bowl, mix together the olive oil, garlic, salt, chili powder, lemon juice, and cilantro. 2. Place the tuna steaks in the mixture, turning the steaks to coat them on all sides. Cover loosely and set aside to marinate the tuna steaks for 20 minutes. 3. Place the Crisper Tray in the bottom position. Add the tuna steaks to it without the marinade and close the lid. 4. Move SmartSwitch to AIR FRY/STOVETOP, set the cooking temperature to 380 degrees F and the cooking time to 7 minutes. 5. Let the dish rest for 5 minutes. 6. Place the tuna steaks on plates, top the fillets with the lemon slices, and serve.

Per Serving: Calories 135; Fat: 1.37g; Sodium: 217mg; Carbs: 1.26g; Fiber: 0.1g; Sugar: 0.36g; Protein: 27.8g

Flavorful Flounder au Gratin

Prep Time: 5 minutes | Cook Time: 15 minutes | Serves: 4

- 4 (6-ounce) flounder fillets
- 4 tablespoons (½ stick) unsalted butter, melted, divided
- ¼ cup whole-wheat panko bread crumbs
- ¼ cup grated Parmesan cheese
- ½ teaspoon salt
- ½ teaspoon dried oregano
- ½ teaspoon dried basil
- ¼ teaspoon freshly ground black pepper
- 1 lemon, quartered
- 1 tablespoon chopped fresh parsley

1. Pat the fish fillets dry and brush them with 2 tablespoons of butter, making sure to coat them on all sides. 2. In a small bowl, mix together the remaining 2 tablespoons of butter, bread crumbs, Parmesan cheese, salt, oregano, basil, and pepper until it becomes a moist but crumbly mixture. 3. Dredge the fish in the bread crumb mixture, making sure to press the crumbs onto the fish, until well coated. 4. Place the Crisper Tray in the bottom position. Add the fillets to it and close the lid. 5. Move SmartSwitch to AIR FRY/STOVETOP, set the cooking temperature to 375 degrees F and the cooking time to 12 minutes. Flip the fillets halfway through. 6. The fillets should be golden and crispy when cooked. 7. Serve the fillets with lemon wedges and a sprinkle of fresh parsley.

Per Serving: Calories 230; Fat: 12.39g; Sodium: 1152mg; Carbs: 8.21g; Fiber: 0.4g; Sugar: 0.35g; Protein: 21.02g

Haddock Fish Fingers

Prep Time: 10 minutes | Cook Time: 10 minutes | Serves: 4

- ¼ cup whole-wheat flour
- ¼ teaspoon salt
- ¼ teaspoon freshly ground black pepper
- ¼ teaspoon smoked paprika
- ¼ teaspoon dried oregano
- 1 egg
- 1 teaspoon water
- 4 (4-ounce) haddock fillets
- 1 lemon, thinly sliced (optional)
- Malt vinegar, for serving (optional)
- Ketchup, for serving (optional)
- Tartar sauce, for serving (optional)

1. In a wide, shallow bowl, mix together the flour, salt, pepper, paprika, and oregano. 2. In a separate wide shallow bowl, whisk together the egg and water. 3. Pat the haddock dry and cut each fillet into 4 strips. Dip each strip into the egg first, letting any excess drip off, and then in the flour mixture until coated on all sides. 4. Place the Crisper Tray in the bottom position. Add the fish to it and close the lid. 5. Move SmartSwitch to AIR FRY/STOVETOP, set the cooking temperature to 400 degrees F and the cooking time to 8 minutes. Flip the food halfway through. 6. Serve the fish with sliced lemon, vinegar, ketchup, or tartar sauce if desired.

Per Serving: Calories 185; Fat: 2.13g; Sodium: 572mg; Carbs: 5.71g; Fiber: 0.9g; Sugar: 0.09g; Protein: 33.91g

Salmon with Tomatoes and Olives

Prep Time: 5 minutes | Cook Time: 8 minutes | Serves: 4:

2 tablespoons olive oil
4 (1½-inch-thick) salmon fillets
½ teaspoon salt
¼ teaspoon cayenne
1 teaspoon chopped fresh dill
2 Roma tomatoes, diced
¼ cup sliced Kalamata olives
4 lemon slices

1. Brush the olive oil on both sides of the salmon fillets, and then season them lightly with salt, cayenne, and dill. 2. Place the Crisper Tray in the bottom position. Place the fillets on the tray, then layer the tomatoes and olives over the top. Top each fillet with a lemon slice. 3. Move SmartSwitch to AIR FRY/STOVETOP, and then use the center front arrows to select BAKE/ROAST. Set the cooking temperature to 380 degrees F and the cooking time to 8 minutes. 4. The salmon should reach an internal temperature of 145 degrees F when cooked. 5. Serve warm.

Per Serving: Calories 568; Fat: 22.91g; Sodium: 554mg; Carbs: 6.59g; Fiber: 1.3g; Sugar: 2.84g; Protein: 80.63g

Parmesan Perch

Prep Time: 5 minutes | Cook Time: 10 minutes | Serves: 5

½ teaspoon salt
¼ teaspoon paprika
¼ teaspoon freshly ground black pepper
1 tablespoon chopped fresh dill
¼ cup grated Parmesan cheese
2 tablespoons whole-wheat bread crumbs
4 (4-ounce) ocean perch fillets
Extra-virgin olive oil, in a spray bottle, for greasing
1 lemon, quartered

1. In a wide, shallow bowl, combine the salt, paprika, pepper, dill, Parmesan cheese, and bread crumbs. 2. Dip the fillets in the Parmesan mixture, turning them to coat on all sides. 3. Place the Crisper Tray in the bottom position. Add the fillets to it and spray them with olive oil. 4. Move SmartSwitch to AIR FRY/STOVETOP, set the cooking temperature to 400 degrees F and the cooking time to 9 minutes. 5. The crust should be golden when cooked. 6. Serve the dish with lemon wedges.

Per Serving: Calories 111; Fat: 3.25g; Sodium: 612mg; Carbs: 4.19g; Fiber: 0.5g; Sugar: 0.43g; Protein: 15.95g

Sea Bass with Root Vegetables

Prep Time: 10 minutes | Cook Time: 15 minutes | Serves: 4

1 carrot, diced small	½ teaspoon onion powder
1 parsnip, diced small	2 garlic cloves, minced
1 rutabaga, diced small	1 lemon, sliced, plus additional wedges for serving
¼ cup olive oil	
2 teaspoons salt, divided	
4 sea bass fillets	

1. In a small bowl, toss the carrot, parsnip, and rutabaga with olive oil and 1 teaspoon salt. 2. Lightly season the sea bass with the remaining 1 teaspoon of salt and the onion powder. 3. Place the Crisper Tray in the bottom position. Place the sea bass on the tray. Spread the garlic over the top of each fillet, then cover with lemon slices. Pour the prepared vegetables into the basket around and on top of the fish. 4. Move SmartSwitch to AIR FRY/STOVETOP, and then use the center front arrows to select BAKE/ROAST. Set the cooking temperature to 380 degrees F and the cooking time to 15 minutes. 5. Serve the sea bass with additional lemon wedges if desired.

Per Serving: Calories 302; Fat: 16.35g; Sodium: 1270mg; Carbs: 13.7g; Fiber: 3g; Sugar: 4.99g; Protein: 25.11g

Shrimp Pita

Prep Time: 5 minutes | Cook Time: 8 minutes | Serves: 4

1 pound medium shrimp, peeled and deveined	¼ teaspoon black pepper
2 tablespoons olive oil	4 whole wheat pitas
1 teaspoon dried oregano	4 ounces feta cheese, crumbled
½ teaspoon dried thyme	1 cup shredded lettuce
½ teaspoon garlic powder	1 tomato, diced
¼ teaspoon onion powder	¼ cup black olives, sliced
½ teaspoon salt	1 lemon

1. In a medium bowl, combine the shrimp with the olive oil, oregano, thyme, garlic powder, onion powder, salt, and black pepper. 2. Place the Crisper Tray in the bottom position. Place the shrimp on the tray and close the lid. 3. Move SmartSwitch to AIR FRY/STOVETOP, and then use the center front arrows to select BAKE/ROAST. Set the cooking temperature to 380 degrees F and the cooking time to 8 minutes. 4. Divide the shrimp into warmed pitas with feta, lettuce, tomato, olives, and a squeeze of lemon.

Per Serving: Calories 303; Fat: 14.8g; Sodium: 1320mg; Carbs: 20.64g; Fiber: 2.9g; Sugar: 2.66g; Protein: 22.83g

Lemon-Pepper Trout Fillets

Prep Time: 5 minutes | Cook Time: 15 minutes | Serves: 4

- 4 trout fillets
- 2 tablespoons olive oil
- ½ teaspoon salt
- 1 teaspoon black pepper
- 2 garlic cloves, sliced
- 1 lemon, sliced, plus additional wedges for serving

1. Brush each fillet with olive oil on both sides and season with salt and pepper. 2. Place the Crisper Tray in the bottom position. Place the fillets on the tray and close the lid. 3. Move SmartSwitch to AIR FRY/STOVETOP, and then use the center front arrows to select BAKE/ROAST. Set the cooking temperature to 380 degrees F and the cooking time to 15 minutes. 4. The salmon should reach an internal temperature of 145 degrees F when cooked. 5. Serve the fillets with fresh lemon wedges.

Per Serving: Calories 183; Fat: 12.03g; Sodium: 332mg; Carbs: 1.79g; Fiber: 0.3g; Sugar: 0.32g; Protein: 16.62g

Chapter 7 Dessert Recipes

Egg Nut Bars 86

Zucchini Bread 86

Orange Muffins with Poppy Seeds 87

Simple Lemon Pie 87

Cream Scones 88

Easy-Baked Apples 88

Filled Apple Pies 89

Amaretto Poached Pears 89

Smith Apple Wedges 90

Butter Banana Bread Pudding 90

Filled Cherry-Berry Crisp 91

Yummy Chocolate Cake 91

Blueberry Muffins 92

Original Cake for One 92

Coconut Cake with Pineapple Topping ... 93

Orange Dundee Cake 93

Delicious Gingerbread 94

Fruit Pockets 94

Apple Blueberry Crumble 95

Simple Coco Whip 95

Fruit Cobbler 96

Cherries Jubilee 96

Walnuts Bread Pudding 97

Caramelized Fruit Nut Topping 97

Egg Nut Bars

Prep Time: 15 minutes | Cook Time: 30 minutes | Serves: 10

½ cup coconut oil, softened
1 teaspoon baking powder
1 teaspoon lemon juice
1 cup almond flour
½ cup coconut flour
3 tablespoons Erythritol
1 teaspoon vanilla extract
2 eggs, beaten
2 oz. hazelnuts, chopped
1 oz. macadamia nuts, chopped
Cooking spray

1. In a suitable baking pan, mix up coconut oil and baking powder. 2. Add lemon juice, almond flour, coconut flour, Erythritol, vanilla extract, and eggs. Stir the mixture until it is smooth or use the immersion blender for this step. 3. Then add hazelnuts and macadamia nuts. Stir the mixture until homogenous. 4. Place the Crisper Tray in the bottom position. Place the pan on the tray, then pour in the nut mixture and flatten it well with the help of the spatula. 5. Move SmartSwitch to AIR FRY/STOVETOP, and then use the center front arrows to select BAKE/ROAST. Set the cooking temperature to 325 degrees F and the cooking time to 30 minutes. 6. Then Cool the mixture well and cut it into the serving bars.

Per Serving: Calories 181; Fat: 18.51g; Sodium: 34mg; Carbs: 2.34g; Fiber: 1g; Sugar: 0.89g; Protein: 2.98g

Zucchini Bread

Prep Time: 10 minutes | Cook Time: 40 minutes | Serves: 12

2 cups almond flour
2 teaspoons baking powder
¾ cup swerve
½ cup coconut oil, melted
1 teaspoon lemon juice
1 teaspoon vanilla extract
3 eggs, whisked
1 cup zucchini, shredded
1 tablespoon lemon zest
Cooking spray

1. In a bowl, mix all the ingredients except the cooking spray and stir well. 2. Grease a loaf pan that fits the air fryer with the cooking spray, line the pan with parchment paper and pour the loaf mix inside. 3. Place the Crisper Tray in the bottom position. Place the pan on the tray and close the lid. 4. Move SmartSwitch to AIR FRY/STOVETOP, and then use the center front arrows to select BAKE/ROAST. Set the cooking temperature to 330 degrees F and the cooking time to 40 minutes. 5. Cool the bread before slicing and serving.

Per Serving: Calories 114; Fat: 11.6g; Sodium: 26mg; Carbs: 0.88g; Fiber: 0.1g; Sugar: 0.26g; Protein: 2.32g

Orange Muffins with Poppy Seeds

Prep Time: 10 minutes | Cook Time: 10 minutes | Serves: 5

5 eggs, beaten
1 tablespoon poppy seeds
1 teaspoon vanilla extract
¼ teaspoon ground nutmeg
½ teaspoon baking powder
1 teaspoon orange juice
1 teaspoon orange zest, grated
5 tablespoons coconut flour
1 tablespoon Monk fruit
2 tablespoons coconut flakes
Cooking spray

1. In the mixing bowl, mix up eggs, poppy seeds, vanilla extract, ground nutmeg, baking powder, orange juice, orange zest, coconut flour, and Monk fruit. 2. Add coconut flakes and mix up the mixture until it is homogenous and without any clumps. 3. Spray the muffin molds with cooking spray from inside. Pour the muffin batter in the molds. 4. Place the Crisper Tray in the bottom position. Place the molds on the tray and close the lid. 5. Move SmartSwitch to AIR FRY/STOVETOP, and then use the center front arrows to select BAKE/ROAST. Set the cooking temperature to 360 degrees F and the cooking time to 10 minutes. 6. Serve and enjoy.

Per Serving: Calories 91; Fat: 5.59g; Sodium: 86mg; Carbs: 3.69g; Fiber: 0.8g; Sugar: 2.22g; Protein: 6.05g

Simple Lemon Pie

Prep Time: 10 minutes | Cook Time: 35 minutes | Serves: 8

2 eggs, whisked
¾ cup swerve
¼ cup coconut flour
2 tablespoons butter, melted
1 teaspoon lemon zest, grated
1 teaspoon baking powder
1 teaspoon vanilla extract
½ teaspoon lemon extract
4 ounces coconut, shredded
Cooking spray

1. In a bowl, combine all the ingredients except the cooking spray and stir well. 2. Grease a suitable pie pan with the cooking spray, pour the mixture inside. 3. Place the Crisper Tray in the bottom position. Place the pan on the tray and close the lid. 4. Move SmartSwitch to AIR FRY/STOVETOP, and then use the center front arrows to select BAKE/ROAST. Set the cooking temperature to 360 degrees F and the cooking time to 35 minutes. 5. Slice and serve warm.

Per Serving: Calories 48; Fat: 3.97g; Sodium: 62mg; Carbs: 1.31g; Fiber: 0.3g; Sugar: 0.7g; Protein: 1.57g

Cream Scones

Prep Time: 20 minutes | Cook Time: 10 minutes | Serves: 4

4 oz. almond flour
½ teaspoon baking powder
1 teaspoon lemon juice
¼ teaspoon salt
2 teaspoons cream cheese
¼ cup coconut cream
1 teaspoon vanilla extract
1 tablespoon Erythritol
1 tablespoon heavy cream
Cooking spray

1. In the mixing bowl, mix up almond flour, baking powder, lemon juice, and salt. 2. Add cream cheese and stir the mixture gently. Mix up vanilla extract and coconut cream in the separated bowl. 3. Add the coconut cream mixture in the almond flour mixture. Stir it gently and then knead the dough. Roll up the dough and cut it on scones. 4. Place the Crisper Tray in the bottom position. Place the scones on the tray and close the lid. 5. Move SmartSwitch to AIR FRY/STOVETOP, and then use the center front arrows to select BAKE/ROAST. Set the cooking temperature to 360 degrees F and the cooking time to 10 minutes. 6. Cool the scones to the room temperature. 7. Meanwhile, mix up heavy cream and Erythritol. Then brush every scone with a sweet cream mixture. Enjoy.

Per Serving: Calories 238; Fat: 21.47g; Sodium: 159mg; Carbs: 7.81g; Fiber: 3.9g; Sugar: 1.59g; Protein: 6.8g

Easy-Baked Apples

Prep Time: 10 minutes | Cook Time: 20 minutes | Serves: 6

3 small honey crisp or other baking apples
3 tablespoons chopped pecans
3 tablespoons pure maple syrup
1 tablespoon vegan butter, divided

1. Wash and dry the apples and cut each in half. 2. Core the halves and remove about a tablespoon of the apple flesh to make a cavity to hold the pecans. 3. Pour ½ cup of water in the pot and place in the Crisper Tray in the bottom position. Place the apple halves on the tray. Into the cavity of each apple, spoon 1½ teaspoons of pecans and ½ tablespoon maple syrup. Top each apple half with ½ teaspoon vegan butter. 4. Move SmartSwitch to RAPID COOKER, and then use the center front arrows to select STEAM. 5. Cook the food for 20 minutes until the apples become soft and tender.

Per Serving: Calories 106; Fat: 4.64g; Sodium: 31mg; Carbs: 17.44g; Fiber: 2.1g; Sugar: 13.92g; Protein: 0.53g

Filled Apple Pies

Prep Time: 30 minutes | Cook Time: 20 minutes | Serves: 4

Dough

2¼ cups self-rising flour, divided

¼ cup all-vegetable shortening

¾ cup almond milk

Filling

4 cups peeled, cored, and diced apples

1 tablespoon lemon juice

1 cup sugar

1 tablespoon cornstarch

1 teaspoon cinnamon

Oil for misting or cooking spray

1. Add 2 cups of the flour to a medium bowl. 2. Cut the shortening into the flour. 3. Stir in the almond milk and set the dough aside while you prepare the apples. 4. Dice the apples into ¼-inch cubes, place them in another medium bowl, add the lemon juice to prevent browning, and stir to coat evenly. 5. In a small bowl, mix the sugar, cornstarch, and cinnamon. 6. Pour the dry ingredients over the apples and stir to coat. 7. Sprinkle remaining ¼ cup flour on a sheet of wax paper. 8. Divide the dough into 12 equal-size balls. 9. On flour-covered wax paper, roll each ball into a thin circle about 5 inches in diameter. 10. Spoon approximately 1½ tablespoons of apple filling onto one side of a dough circle. 11. With a finger dipped in water, moisten the inside edge of the dough circle all around. 12. Fold the dough over to make a half-moon, seal, and crimp the edges with a fork. 13. Repeat steps 10 through 12 with 3 more dough circles. 14. Mist each pie on both sides with oil or cooking spray. 15. Place the Crisper Tray in the bottom position. Place the pies on the tray and close the lid. 16. Move SmartSwitch to AIR FRY/STOVETOP, and then use the center front arrows to select BAKE/ROAST. Set the cooking temperature to 360 degrees F and the cooking time to 20 minutes. 17. You can cook the pies in batches.

Per Serving: Calories 549; Fat: 14.27g; Sodium: 873mg; Carbs: 99.02g; Fiber: 5.1g; Sugar: 39.98g; Protein: 7.57g

Amaretto Poached Pears

Prep Time: 10 minutes | Cook Time: 15 minutes | Serves: 3-4

½ cup amaretto liqueur

½ cup water

2 fresh pears

1. Pour the amaretto and water in a suitable baking pan. 2. Cut the pears in half lengthwise. 3. Peel and core the pears, then slice them crosswise into ½-inch slices. 4. Stir the pears into the diluted amaretto. 5. Place the Crisper Tray in the bottom position. Place the pan on the tray and close the lid. 6. Move SmartSwitch to AIR FRY/STOVETOP, and then use the center front arrows to select BAKE/ROAST. Set the cooking temperature to 360 degrees F and the cooking time to 15 minutes. 7. Cool the dish to room temperature or chill in syrup.

Per Serving: Calories 143; Fat: 0.24g; Sodium: 3mg; Carbs: 22.78g; Fiber: 2.2g; Sugar: 17.63g; Protein: 0.34g

Smith Apple Wedges

Prep Time: 10 minutes | Cook Time: 5 minutes | Serves: 4

- 1 tablespoon Bob's Red Mill egg replacer
- 5 tablespoons water
- ¼ cup panko breadcrumbs
- ¼ cup finely chopped peanuts
- 1 teaspoon coconut sugar
- 1 teaspoon cocoa powder
- 1 teaspoon cinnamon
- ¼ cup potato starch
- 1 medium Granny Smith apple
- Oil for misting or cooking spray

1. In a shallow dish, mix the egg replacer and water and set aside to thicken. 2. In another shallow dish, mix together the breadcrumbs, peanuts, sugar, cocoa, and cinnamon. 3. In a resealable plastic bag or a container with a lid, place the potato starch. 4. Cut the apple into small wedges. The thickest edge should be no more than ⅜- to ½-inch thick. Cut away the core but don't peel. 5. Place the apple wedges in the potato starch and shake to coat. 6. Dip the wedges in egg wash, shake off the excess, and roll them in the crumb mixture. 7. Spray the wedges with oil or cooking spray. 8. Place the Crisper Tray in the bottom position. Place the apple wedges on the tray and close the lid. 9. Move SmartSwitch to AIR FRY/STOVETOP, and then use the center front arrows to select BAKE/ROAST. Set the cooking temperature to 390 degrees F and the cooking time to 5 minutes. 10. The cocoa will make the coating look dark, but you'll see the peanut chunks turn golden brown. 11. Serve hot.

Per Serving: Calories 169; Fat: 7.64g; Sodium: 150mg; Carbs: 20.14g; Fiber: 3.1g; Sugar: 6.82g; Protein: 6.65g

Butter Banana Bread Pudding

Prep Time: 10 minutes | Cook Time: 25 minutes | Serves: 4-6

- 1 tablespoon Bob's Red Mill egg replacer
- 2 tablespoons water
- Cooking spray
- 1 cup all-purpose white flour
- 1 teaspoon baking powder
- ¼ teaspoon salt
- ¾ cup mashed ripe banana
- ¼ cup peanut butter
- ¼ cup almond milk
- ¼ cup pure maple syrup
- 2 tablespoons coconut oil
- ½ teaspoon pure vanilla extract

1. In a small bowl, mix the egg replacer and water and set aside for 1 minute to thicken. 2. Spray a suitable baking dish lightly with cooking spray. 3. In a medium bowl, mix together the flour, baking powder, and salt. 4. In a separate mixing bowl, combine the banana, peanut butter, milk, maple syrup, coconut oil, vanilla, and egg mixture and mix well. 5. Gently stir the banana mixture into the dry ingredients. Blend well but don't beat. The batter will feel very thick. Spread the batter evenly in the prepared baking pan. 6. Place the Crisper Tray in the bottom position. Place the pan on the tray and close the lid. 7. Move SmartSwitch to AIR FRY/STOVETOP, and then use the center front arrows to select BAKE/ROAST. Set the cooking temperature to 330 degrees F and the cooking time to 22 minutes. 8. The pudding is done when the top has browned and feels firm when pressed with the back of a spoon.

Per Serving: Calories 212; Fat: 8.2g; Sodium: 269mg; Carbs: 31.54g; Fiber: 1.1g; Sugar: 12.44g; Protein: 3.51g

Filled Cherry-Berry Crisp

Prep Time: 10 minutes | Cook Time: 10 minutes | Serves: 4

Filling

Cooking spray

1 (10-ounce) bag frozen cherries, thawed and undrained

1 cup fresh blueberries

¼ cup coconut sugar

2 tablespoons amaretto liqueur

Topping

2 tablespoons oats

2 tablespoons oat bran

¼ cup cooked quinoa

2 tablespoons sliced almonds

2 tablespoons coconut sugar

2 teaspoons coconut oil

1. Spray a suitable baking pan with nonstick cooking spray. 2. Combine all filling ingredients in the baking pan and stir well. 3. In a medium bowl, combine all of the topping ingredients and mix until the oil is distributed evenly and the mixture is crumbly. 4. Spoon the topping evenly over the filling in the pan. 5. Place the Crisper Tray in the bottom position. Place the pan on the tray and close the lid. 6. Move SmartSwitch to AIR FRY/STOVETOP, and then use the center front arrows to select BAKE/ROAST. Set the cooking temperature to 360 degrees F and the cooking time to 9 minutes. 7. The crumb topping should turn golden brown and crispy when cooked. 8. Serve and enjoy.

Per Serving: Calories 240; Fat: 3.52g; Sodium: 5mg; Carbs: 50.77g; Fiber: 3.8g; Sugar: 41.02g; Protein: 2.9g

Yummy Chocolate Cake

Prep Time: 10 minutes | Cook Time: 30 minutes | Serves: 8:

Oil for misting or cooking spray

1 tablespoon Bob's Red Mill egg replacer

2 tablespoons water

½ cup sugar

¼ cup self-rising flour, plus 3 tablespoons

3 tablespoons cocoa

¼ teaspoon baking soda

¼ teaspoon salt

2 tablespoons vegan oil

1 (5.3-ounce) container vegan vanilla yogurt

¼ cup nut milk of choice

1. Spray the baking pan with oil and set aside. 2. In a medium bowl, using a wire whisk, whisk together the egg replacer and water. 3. Add the remaining ingredients and whisk until smooth. 4. Pour the batter into the baking pan. 5. Place the Crisper Tray in the bottom position. Place the pan on the tray and close the lid. 6. Move SmartSwitch to AIR FRY/STOVETOP, and then use the center front arrows to select BAKE/ROAST. Set the cooking temperature to 330 degrees F and the cooking time to 30 minutes. 7. The toothpick inserted into the center should come out clean when cooked. 8. Let the cake rest for 10 minutes before removing it from the pan. Enjoy.

Per Serving: Calories 117; Fat: 4.39g; Sodium: 235mg; Carbs: 15.44g; Fiber: 0.6g; Sugar: 9.88g; Protein: 4.2g

Blueberry Muffins

Prep Time: 10 minutes | Cook Time: 18 minutes | Serves: 6

- 1 cup finely ground blanched almond flour
- ⅓ cup Swerve Confectioners sweetener
- 1½ teaspoons baking powder
- ½ teaspoon baking soda
- ¼ teaspoon sea salt
- ¼ teaspoon xanthan gum
- 1 large egg, beaten
- ½ cup sour cream
- 2 tablespoons heavy (whipping) cream
- 1 teaspoon pure vanilla extract
- ½ cup fresh or frozen blueberries
- Almond Glaze (optional)

1. In a large bowl, combine the almond flour, Swerve, baking powder, baking soda, sea salt, and xanthan gum. 2. In a medium bowl, whisk together the egg, sour cream, heavy cream, and vanilla. 3. Add the wet ingredients to the dry ingredients, and stir until just combined. Gently stir in the blueberries. 4. Divide the batter among 6 silicone muffin cups. 5. Place the Crisper Tray in the bottom position. Place the muffin cups on the tray and close the lid. 6. Move SmartSwitch to AIR FRY/STOVETOP, and then use the center front arrows to select BAKE/ROAST. Set the cooking temperature to 300 degrees F and the cooking time to 18 minutes. 7. Drizzle with the almond glaze (if using) before serving.

Per Serving: Calories 249; Fat: 17.51g; Sodium: 239mg; Carbs: 18.47g; Fiber: 3.7g; Sugar: 10.74g; Protein: 7.11g

Original Cake for One

Prep Time: 10 minutes | Cook Time: 10 minutes | Serves: 1

- 3 tablespoons unbleached all-purpose flour
- 1½ tablespoons cocoa powder
- 1 tablespoon plus 1 teaspoon sugar
- ¼ teaspoon baking powder
- ⅛ teaspoon salt
- 3 teaspoons applesauce
- 3 tablespoons almond milk
- ½ teaspoon vanilla extract
- 1 to 2 spritzes canola oil
- Simple Coco Whip, for serving (optional)

1. In a medium bowl, combine the flour, cocoa powder, sugar, baking powder, and salt. 2. In a small bowl, combine the applesauce, milk, and vanilla. Pour the applesauce mixture over the flour mixture and stir until there are no lumps in the batter. 3. Spritz a small ramekin with the oil. Pour the batter into the ramekin. 4. Place the Crisper Tray in the bottom position. Place the ramekin on the tray and close the lid. 5. Move SmartSwitch to AIR FRY/STOVETOP, and then use the center front arrows to select BAKE/ROAST. Set the cooking temperature to 360 degrees F and the cooking time to 10 minutes. 6. The cake is done when you insert a toothpick into the center and it comes out clean. Serve the cooled cake with the coco whip, if desired.

Per Serving: Calories 162; Fat: 3.68g; Sodium: 333mg; Carbs: 29.81g; Fiber: 3.2g; Sugar: 6.62g; Protein: 5.33g

Coconut Cake with Pineapple Topping

Prep Time: 10 minutes | Cook Time: 35 minutes | Serves: 8

- Cooking spray
- 1 tablespoon Bob's Red Mill egg replacer
- 2 tablespoons water
- ½ cup sugar
- 1½ cups self-rising flour
- 2 tablespoons coconut oil
- 1 cup coconut milk
- ½ cup unsweetened flaked coconut

Pineapple Lime Topping
- 1 (8-ounce) can crushed pineapple in juice, drained
- 1 teaspoon grated lime zest
- 1 tablespoon lime juice
- 1¼ cups sugar

1. Spray the baking pan with nonstick spray and set aside. 2. In a medium bowl, using a wire whisk, whisk together the egg replacer and water. 3. Add the sugar, flour, coconut oil, and coconut milk and whisk until blended. Stir in the coconut. 4. Pour the batter into the prepared pan. 5. Place the Crisper Tray in the bottom position. Place the pan on the tray and close the lid. 6. Move SmartSwitch to AIR FRY/STOVETOP, and then use the center front arrows to select BAKE/ROAST. Set the cooking temperature to 330 degrees F and the cooking time to 35 minutes. 7. A toothpick inserted into the center should come out with soft crumbs attached. 8. Let the cake rest in the pan for 10 minutes before removing it. 9. While the cake is baking, prepare the topping. In a small saucepan over medium-high heat, combine all of the topping ingredients. 10. Bring the topping to a boil, stirring constantly, boil for 1 minute and then remove from the heat. 11. Let the topping cool and serve it at room temperature.

Per Serving: Calories 276; Fat: 5.19g; Sodium: 311mg; Carbs: 54.07g; Fiber: 1g; Sugar: 35.79g; Protein: 4.07g

Orange Dundee Cake

Prep Time: 16 minutes | Cook Time: 30 minutes | Serves: 8

- Cooking spray
- 2 tablespoons Bob's Red Mill egg replacer
- 4 tablespoons water
- 4 tablespoons coconut oil
- ½ cup sugar
- 1 cup dried currants
- ⅓ cup slivered almonds
- 1 tablespoon grated orange peel
- 1 tablespoon grated lemon peel
- 1 cup self-rising flour
- ½ cup almond flour
- 2 tablespoons orange juice, orange liqueur, or brandy

1. Spray the baking pan with nonstick cooking spray. 2. In a large bowl, mix together the egg replacer and water. Stir in the coconut oil and sugar and beat until smooth. 3. Add flours, almonds, currants, lemon and orange peels, and orange juice or liqueur or brandy. 4. Pour the batter into the baking pan, smoothing the top. 5. BAKE the food at 330 degrees F for 30 minutes until toothpick inserted into the center comes out with moist crumbs. 6. Serve and enjoy.

Per Serving: Calories 163; Fat: 8.11g; Sodium: 189mg; Carbs: 20.71g; Fiber: 1.2g; Sugar: 7.56g; Protein: 2.44g

Chapter 7 Dessert Recipes | 93

Delicious Gingerbread

Prep Time: 15 minutes | Cook Time: 20 minutes | Serves: 4-8

1½ teaspoons lemon juice
Scant ½ cup almond milk
1 tablespoon Bob's Red Mill egg replacer
2 tablespoons water
Cooking spray
1 cup all-purpose white flour
2 tablespoons coconut sugar
¾ teaspoon ground ginger
¼ teaspoon cinnamon
1 teaspoon baking powder
½ teaspoon baking soda
⅛ teaspoon salt
¼ cup molasses
2 tablespoons extra-light olive oil
1 teaspoon pure vanilla extract

1. Pour the lemon juice into a glass measuring cup. 2. Add enough almond milk to measure ½ cup. 3. In a small cup, mix the egg replacer and water and set aside. 4. Spray a suitable baking pan lightly with cooking spray. 5. In a medium bowl, mix together all of the dry ingredients. Add the molasses, olive oil, vanilla extract, and egg replacer mixture to the almond milk and stir until well mixed. 6. Pour the liquid mixture into the dry ingredients and stir until well blended. 7. Pour the batter into the baking pan. 8. Place the Crisper Tray in the bottom position. Place the pan on the tray and close the lid. 9. Move SmartSwitch to AIR FRY/STOVETOP, and then use the center front arrows to select BAKE/ROAST. Set the cooking temperature to 330 degrees F and the cooking time to 20 minutes. 10. A toothpick inserted into the center of the loaf should come out clean when done.

Per Serving: Calories 142; Fat: 4.24g; Sodium: 134mg; Carbs: 23.89g; Fiber: 0.6g; Sugar: 11.29g; Protein: 2.03g

Fruit Pockets

Prep Time: 10 minutes | Cook Time: 15 minutes | Serves: 4

1 to 2 teaspoons sugar over the crescent roll dough before rolling it out.
4 ounces vegan crescent roll dough
1 tablespoon unbleached all-purpose flour
6 ounces fresh blueberries, strawberries, or blackberries
½ teaspoon granulated sugar
¼ teaspoon ground cardamom
¼ teaspoon ground ginger
1 teaspoon powdered sugar

1. Divide the crescent roll dough into 4 equal parts. Sprinkle the flour on a work surface and roll the dough pieces out to 5 x 5-inch pieces, using more flour as needed to avoid sticking. 2. In a medium bowl, combine the blueberries, sugar, cardamom, and ginger. 3. Spoon about ⅓ cup of the blueberry mixture onto each piece of dough. 4. Fold each corner toward the center. Work the edges of the dough to ensure it's sealed; it will resemble a pocket. 5. Place the Crisper Tray in the bottom position. Place the pockets on the tray and close the lid. 6. Move SmartSwitch to AIR FRY/STOVETOP, and then use the center front arrows to select BAKE/ROAST. Set the cooking temperature to 360 degrees F and the cooking time to 7 minutes. 7. Sprinkle the powdered sugar on the pastry pockets before serving.

Per Serving: Calories 130; Fat: 1.24g; Sodium: 143mg; Carbs: 26.83g; Fiber: 1.4g; Sugar: 12.06g; Protein: 3.3g

Apple Blueberry Crumble

Prep Time: 10 minutes | Cook Time: 20 minutes | Serves: 2

- 1 medium apple, finely diced
- ½ cup frozen blueberries, strawberries, or peaches
- ¼ cup plus 1 tablespoon brown rice flour
- 2 tablespoons sugar
- ½ teaspoon ground cinnamon
- 2 tablespoons nondairy butter

1. Combine the apple and frozen blueberries in an air fryer–safe baking pan or ramekin. 2. In a small bowl, combine the flour, sugar, cinnamon, and butter. Spoon the flour mixture over the fruit. Sprinkle a little extra flour over everything to cover any exposed fruit. 3. BAKE the food at 350 degrees F for 15 minutes. 4. Serve and enjoy.

Per Serving: Calories 273; Fat: 12.48g; Sodium: 94mg; Carbs: 40.9g; Fiber: 4.5g; Sugar: 20.74g; Protein: 1.97g

Simple Coco Whip

Prep Time: 10 minutes | Cook Time: 20 minutes | Serves: 4

- 1 (13-ounce) can full-fat coconut milk
- 1 tablespoon sugar
- 1 teaspoon vanilla extract

1. Refrigerate the can of coconut milk overnight. 2. Open the can and scoop out the solid cream into a stand mixer bowl or mixing bowl if you are using an electric mixer. 3. Beat the coconut cream on high speed until stiff peaks are formed 4. Add the sugar and vanilla and beat for 1 minute longer. Serve immediately.

Per Serving: Calories 223; Fat: 21.97g; Sodium: 14mg; Carbs: 7.23g; Fiber: 2g; Sugar: 5.17g; Protein: 2.11g

Fruit Cobbler

Prep Time: 10 minutes | Cook Time: 8 minutes | Serves: 1

½ cup chopped frozen peaches or blueberries
½ cup granola or muesli
½ teaspoon cold nondairy butter, cut into small cubes

1. Layer the peaches, granola, and butter in a small casserole dish. Cover the dish with a heatproof lid or foil. 2. Place the Crisper Tray in the bottom position. Place the dish on the tray and close the lid. 3. Move SmartSwitch to AIR FRY/STOVETOP, and then use the center front arrows to select BAKE/ROAST. Set the cooking temperature to 390 degrees F and the cooking time to 8 minutes. 4. Remove the cover after 6 minutes of cooking time.

Per Serving: Calories 97; Fat: 4.22g; Sodium: 46mg; Carbs: 14.11g; Fiber: 1.7g; Sugar: 9.46g; Protein: 1.78g

Cherries Jubilee

Prep Time: 10 minutes | Cook Time: 10 minutes | Serves: 2-4

2 tablespoons nondairy butter
2 cups fresh cherries, pitted and halved
2 tablespoons sugar

1. Melt the butter in a microwave. 2. In a medium bowl, toss the cherries with the butter and sugar. 3. Transfer the cherries to a small baking pan. 4. Place the Crisper Tray in the bottom position. Place the pan on the tray and close the lid. 5. Move SmartSwitch to AIR FRY/STOVETOP, and then use the center front arrows to select BAKE/ROAST. Set the cooking temperature to 350 degrees F and the cooking time to 10 minutes. 6. Toss the food halfway through the cooking time. 7. Transfer the cherries to a bowl and allow them to cool.

Per Serving: Calories 110; Fat: 5.9g; Sodium: 46mg; Carbs: 15.04g; Fiber: 1.4g; Sugar: 12.76g; Protein: 0.79g

Walnuts Bread Pudding

Prep Time: 10 minutes | Cook Time: 20 minutes | Serves: 4

- 2 cups cubed day-old bread (a French baguette or sourdough bread is ideal)
- 1 ½ cups soymilk
- 1 tablespoon sugar
- ¼ teaspoon vanilla extract
- ½ teaspoon ground cinnamon
- ¼ cup golden raisins
- ¼ cup dried currants
- ¼ cup finely chopped walnuts

1. Place the bread in a medium bowl. 2. In a small bowl, combine the milk, sugar, vanilla, cinnamon, raisins, currants, and walnuts. 3. Pour the milk mixture over the bread and mix well. 4. Transfer the mixture to a suitable baking pan that fits into the basket. 5. Place the Crisper Tray in the bottom position. Place the pan on the tray and close the lid. 6. Move SmartSwitch to AIR FRY/STOVETOP, and then use the center front arrows to select BAKE/ROAST. Set the cooking temperature to 360 degrees F and the cooking time to 20 minutes. 7. Remove the bread pudding and let it cool for 20 to 30 minutes before serving.

Per Serving: Calories 151; Fat: 4.61g; Sodium: 131mg; Carbs: 24g; Fiber: 2g; Sugar: 12.13g; Protein: 4.94g

Caramelized Fruit Nut Topping

Prep Time: 10 minutes | Cook Time: 20 minutes | Serves: 4

- 1 teaspoon sugar
- 1 teaspoon light agave syrup
- 1 teaspoon nondairy butter
- ½ cup coarsely chopped walnuts
- ½ cup coarsely chopped pecans
- ½ cup coarsely chopped dried apricots, cherries, cranberries, or raisins
- ¼ teaspoon ground cinnamon

1. Combine the sugar, agave syrup, and butter in a suitable baking pan. 2. Add the walnuts, pecans, apricots, and cinnamon, and toss them well. 3. Place the Crisper Tray in the bottom position. Place the pan on the tray and close the lid. 4. Move SmartSwitch to AIR FRY/STOVETOP, and then use the center front arrows to select BAKE/ROAST. Set the cooking temperature to 390 degrees F and the cooking time to 5 minutes. 5. Stir the food after 3 minutes of cooking time. 6. Serve and enjoy.

Per Serving: Calories 206; Fat: 16.47g; Sodium: 11mg; Carbs: 15.39g; Fiber: 3.1g; Sugar: 11.41g; Protein: 3.23g

Conclusion

Are you ready to switch to a healthy lifestyle and embark on your weight loss journey? The Ninja speedi is the perfect choice for you! This incredible 12-in-1 kitchen appliance can air fry, crisp, roast, bake, broil, reheat, and dehydrate meats and vegetables, resulting in healthier desserts and snacks. This all-in-one food appliance eliminates extra fats from the food and gives you your desired level of crispiness. With its dishwasher-safe accessories and easy-to-understand cooking settings, you can now cook for the whole family at once with its high-capacity pot, which can lighten your kitchen workload. And to top it off, it comes with a recommended cookbook to help you whip up delicious, nutritious meals for yourself and your loved ones. So don't wait and start your journey to a healthier lifestyle with the Ninja speedi today!

Appendix 1 Air Fryer Cooking Chart

Frozen Foods	Temp (°F)	Time (min)
Onion Rings (12 oz.)	400	8
Thin French Fries (20 oz.)	400	14
Thick French Fries (17 oz.)	400	18
Pot Sticks (10 oz.)	400	8
Fish Sticks (10 oz.)	400	10
Fish Fillets (½-inch, 10 oz.)	400	14

vegetables	Temp (°F)	Time (min)
Asparagus (1-inch slices)	400	5
Beets (sliced)	350	25
Beets (whole)	400	40
Bell Peppers (sliced)	350	13
Broccoli	400	6
Brussels Sprouts (halved)	380	15
Carrots (½-inch slices)	380	15
Cauliflower (florets)	400	12
Eggplant (1½-inch cubes)	400	15
Fennel (quartered)	370	15
Mushrooms (¼-inch slices)	400	5
Onion (pearl)	400	10
Parsnips (½-inch chunks)	380	5
Peppers (1-inch chunks)	400	15
Potatoes (baked, whole)	400	40
Squash (½-inch chunks)	400	12
Tomatoes (cherry)	400	4
Zucchni (½-inch sticks)	400	12

Meat	Temp (°F)	Time (min)
Bacon	400	5 to 7
Beef Eye Round Roast (4 lbs.)	390	50 to 60
Burger (4 oz.)	370	16 to 20
Chicken Breasts, bone-in (1.25 lbs.)	370	25
Chicken Breasts, boneless (4 oz.)	380	12
Chicken Drumsticks (2.5 lbs.)	370	20
Chicken Thighs, bone-in (2 lbs.)	380	22
Chicken Thighs, boneless (1.5 lbs.)	380	18 to 20
Chicken Legs, bone-in (1.75 lbs.)	380	30
Chicken Wings (2 lbs.)	400	12
Flank Steak (1.5 lbs.)	400	12
Game Hen (halved, 2 lbs.)	390	20
Loin (2 lbs.)	360	55
London Broil (2 lbs.)	400	20 to 28
Meatballs (3-inch)	380	10
Rack of Lamb (1.5-2 lbs.)	380	22
Sausages	380	15
Whole Chicken (6.5 lbs.)	360	75

Fish and Seafood	Temp (°F)	Time (min)
Calamari (8 oz.)	400	4
Fish Fillet (1-inch, 8 oz.)	400	10
Salmon Fillet (6 oz.)	380	12
Tuna Steak	400	7 to 10
Scallops	400	5 to 7
Shrimp	400	5

Appendix 2 Measurement Conversion Chart

WEIGHT EQUIVALENTS

US STANDARD	METRIC (APPROXIMATE)
1 ounce	28 g
2 ounces	57 g
5 ounces	142 g
10 ounces	284 g
15 ounces	425 g
16 ounces (1 pound)	455 g
1.5 pounds	680 g
2 pounds	907 g

VOLUME EQUIVALENTS (DRY)

US STANDARD	METRIC (APPROXIMATE)
⅛ teaspoon	0.5 mL
¼ teaspoon	1 mL
½ teaspoon	2 mL
¾ teaspoon	4 mL
1 teaspoon	5 mL
1 tablespoon	15 mL
¼ cup	59 mL
½ cup	118 mL
¾ cup	177 mL
1 cup	235 mL
2 cups	475 mL
3 cups	700 mL
4 cups	1 L

TEMPERATURES EQUIVALENTS

FAHRENHEIT(F)	CELSIUS(C) (APPROXIMATE)
225 °F	107 °C
250 °F	120 °C
275 °F	135 °C
300 °F	150 °C
325 °F	160 °C
350 °F	180 °C
375 °F	190 °C
400 °F	205 °C
425 °F	220 °C
450 °F	235 °C
475 °F	245 °C
500 °F	260 °C

VOLUME EQUIVALENTS (LIQUID)

US STANDARD	US STANDARD (OUNCES)	METRIC APPROXIMATE)
2 tablespoons	1 fl.oz	30 mL
¼ cup	2 fl.oz	60 mL
½ cup	4 fl.oz	120 mL
1 cup	8 fl.oz	240 mL
1½ cup	12 fl.oz	355 mL
2 cups or 1 pint	16 fl.oz	475 mL
4 cups or 1 quart	32 fl.oz	1 L
1 gallon	128 fl.oz	4 L

Appendix 3 Recipes Index

A

African Pork Shoulder   68
Amaretto Poached Pears   89
Apple Blueberry Crumble   95
Avocado & Black Bean Rolls   44

B

Bacon & Eggs in Avocado   15
Bacon Cheeseburger Casserole   69
Bacon Spinach Muffins   17
Beef Empanadas   63
Beef Tips with Onions   73
Beet Chips   46
Black Olives & Beans Tortillas   36
Blooming Onion with Sauce   46
Blueberry Crepes   23
Blueberry Muffins   92
Boneless Chicken Thighs   55
Broccoli with Garlic Sauce   33
Brussels Sprouts with Bacon   42
Buffalo Cauliflower Bites   49
Buffalo Cauliflower Wings   49
Buffalo Chicken Muffins   18
Butter Banana Bread Pudding   90
Butter Peanut Sticks   24
Butter Pork Tenderloin Chopps   66
Butter Turkey Breast   54

C

Caper Salmon Burgers   79
Caramelized Fruit Nut Topping   97
Cauliflower & Chickpea Salad   28
Cauliflower Casserole   38

Cheese Beef Stuffed Peppers   74
Cheese Black Bean Quesadillas   37
Cheese Bowtie Pasta Bake   37
Cheese Eggplant Casserole   36
Cheese Stuffed Zucchini   31
Cheese Zucchini Rice Fritters   29
Cherries Jubilee 96
Chicken Meatloaf   55
Chili-Lime Tilapia   77
Chinese Cabbage & Peppers Bake 34
Cilantro Butter Mahi Mahi   77
Classic Chicken Kebab   57
Coconut Cake with Pineapple Topping   93
Cod Piccata with Potatoes   79
Colby Cauliflower Fritters   32
Corn Salsa   45
Cream Scones   88
Crispy Brussels Sprout Pieces   43
Crispy Coconut Chips   21
Crusted Avocado Wedges   45
Crusted Pork Tenderloin with Potatoes   65
Crusted Turkey Cutlets   60

D

Deconstructed Chicago Hot Dogs 65
Delicious Corn Fritters   44
Delicious Gingerbread   94
Double-Dipped Cinnamon Biscuits 25

E

Easy Bacon Slices   25

Easy Pork Tenderloin   63
Easy-Baked Apples   88
Egg Nut Bars   86
Egg Onion Pizza   16
English Muffin Sandwich   22

F

Feta Egg Spinach Bake   20
Filled Apple Pies   89
Filled Cherry-Berry Crisp   91
Flavorful Flounder au Gratin   81
Flavorful Tofu & Pineapple   35
Fried Pickles with Dressing   50
Fruit Cobbler   96
Fruit Pockets   94

G

Glazed Baby Back Ribs 66
Green Beans with Sun-Dried Tomatoes   28

H

Haddock Fish Fingers   81
Halloumi Rainbow Omelet   31
Ham Omelet   16
Healthy Scotch Eggs   70
Hearty Celery Croquettes   32
Homemade Cornbread   24
Homemade Fish 'n' Chips   76

J

Jalapeño Poppers Wrapped in Bacon 42

L

Lamb Kofta with Yogurt Sauce   73

Lebanese Malfouf 74
Lemo Tuna Steaks 80
Lemon Chicken Thighs 59
Lemon Mushrooms 41
Lemon-Pepper Trout Fillets 84

M

Meritage Large Eggs 15
Mini Cheese Sandwiches 48
Mozzarella Bell Pepper Salad 29
Mustard Pork Chops 68

O

Onion & Beef Stuffed Peppers 72
Onion Mushroom Burgers 34
Orange Dundee Cake 93
Orange Muffins with Poppy Seeds 87
Original Cake for One 92

P

Parmesan Perch 82
Pecan Oatmeal Bars 23
Pecan Pork Stuffing 67
Pineapple Chicken 56
Pork Chops with Scallions 71
Pork Milanese 69
Portabella Mushroom Strips 26
Potato Oat Muffins 22
Prosciutto-Wrapped Chicken with Squash 53

R

Radish Fries 21
Russet Potato Skins 48

S

Salmon with Tomatoes and Green Beans 80
Salmon with Tomatoes and Olives 82
Sausage Patties 18
Sausages with Peppers and Onions 70
Savory Pork Shoulder 67
Savory Sausage Cobbler 71
Sea Bass with Root Vegetables 83
Seasoned Kale Chips 43
Shrimp Caesar Salad 76
Shrimp Pita 83
Shrimp with Orange Sauce 78
Shrimp with Wild Rice Pilaf 78
Simple Coco Whip 95
Simple Lemon Pie 87
Simple Turkey Meatballs 59
Simple-Spiced Pork Chops 62
Smith Apple Wedges 90
Southwestern Taco 19
Spanish Chicken & Peppers 52
Spanish Rice Taquitos 38
Spiced Chicken Shawarma 58
Spiced Kale Chips 50
Spiced Veggie Frittata 17
Spice-Rubbed Ribeye 64
Spicy Olives 40
Spicy Pecans 41
Spinach Chicken Pizza 58
Steak Salad with Blue Cheese Dressing 72
Steak with Onion Gravy 62
Stuffed Chicken Breasts 56
Stuffed Turkey Meatballs 53
Sweet Potato Chips with Parsley 47

T

Tofu Donut Bites 20
Tofu Kebabs 35
Tomato Bruschetta 47
Turkey Breast Tenderloin 54
Turkey Burgers with Potato Fries 52
Turkey Meatballs 57
Typical Egg Sandwich 19
Tzatziki Lamb Kofta 64

V

Valerie's Sammies 26
Veggie Fritters 33

W

Walnuts Bread Pudding 97
Wonderful Avocado Fries 30

Y

Yummy Chocolate Cake 91

Z

Zucchini Bread 86
Zucchini Chips 40
Zucchini Cubes with Mediterranean Dill Sauce 30

Made in the USA
Columbia, SC
18 April 2023